What's Wrong with My Car?

What's Wrong with My Car?

A Guide to Troubleshooting Common Mechanical and Performance Problems

Based on a *Popular Science* series

Edited by Mort Schultz
with Alfred W. Lees, Ernest V. Heyn,
and the Editors of
Consumer Reports Books

Consumers Union
Mount Vernon, New York

Copyright © 1990 by Ernest V. Heyn, Alfred W. Lees, *Popular Science* magazine, and
Consumers Union of U.S., Inc., Mount Vernon, New York 10553.
All rights reserved, including the right of reproduction
in whole or in part in any form.

Library of Congress Cataloging-in-Publication Data
What's wrong with my car? : a guide to troubleshooting common
mechanical and performance problems / edited by Mort Schultz with
Alfred W. Lees, Ernest V. Heyn, and the editors of Consumer Reports
Books.
   p. cm.
   "Based on a Popular Science series."
   ISBN 0-89043-068-3 (pbk.) : $14.95 (est.)
   1. Automobiles—Maintenance and repair—Amateurs' manuals.
I. Schultz, Morton J. II. Lees, Alfred W. III. Heyn, Ernest
Victor, 1904– . IV. Consumer Reports Books.
TL152.W466 1990
629.28'dc20   89-27413
                                                                      CIP

Designed by Jeffrey L. Ward
First printing, February 1990
Manufactured in the United States of America

Contents

Acknowledgments

The authors wish to thank the writers, editors, and illustrators whose contributions to *Popular Science* magazine have been adapted for this book, in particular Bob Cerullo, Ray Pioch, and Russell Von Sauers. Special thanks to C. P. Gilmore, former editor in chief at *Popular Science,* for his past support for this and other Popular Science books, and to the executives of Times Mirror Magazines, publishers of *Popular Science.*

What's Wrong with My Car?

Introduction

Even an experienced home mechanic needs help pinpointing the reason for a car's poor performance. If ignored and left unrepaired, certain problems can turn into chronic aggravations. Others can lead to a seriously damaged vehicle and big bills from an auto repair shop. *What's Wrong with My Car?* is the competent home mechanic's helper. It takes you step-by-step through the troubleshooting process to help you find out exactly what's wrong.

Based on a series of articles from *Popular Science* magazine, *What's Wrong with My Car?* provides bumper-to-bumper coverage of common problems that you can troubleshoot, including hard starting, detonation and preignition, hesitation and stalling, rough idling, poor fuel economy, overheating, and vibrations. Each chapter tells you what systems to check and how to check them—efficiently, systematically, and safely. Although the book does not go into detail about carburetor and transmission repair or electronic fuel injection, all best left in the hands of very experienced and usually professional mechanics, the information in this book applies to the vast majority of cars now on the road.

How to Use This Book

The book assumes that you have a basic interest in the mechanics of engines and road vehicles. But even if you never pick up a tool to do a procedure yourself, the chapters can give you a detailed understanding of most of the systems of a car. This knowledge is valuable in itself. It can help you deal more confidently with your mechanic when you talk about a problem's symptoms, causes, and repair.

If you do the work yourself, you'll need basic tools such as a set of open-end or box wrenches, a ratchet, socket wrenches, screwdrivers, pliers, and some special troubleshooting tools discussed later. Make certain you have a solid grasp of how your car and the system work. Don't undertake any job if you feel uncertain about your skills or knowledge. When in doubt, seek out professional help.

If you plan to do the work yourself, an additional reference source is essential. To supplement the instructions given in the book, you *must* have the manufacturer's repair manual for the vehicle you own. This book must deal in more general terms, but is always far more accessible than the manufacturer's manual. The manual does not explain why you follow certain procedures in certain situations; that's the job of *What's Wrong with My Car?*

It would pay to browse through the book *before* you encounter any trouble with your car. If you have a specific problem, check the table of contents to find the symptom or system that you need to troubleshoot. A *troubleshooting brief* introduces each chapter;

it summarizes what problems and systems are covered in the chapter. Read the brief to get a general idea of what you'll be dealing with. Some problems may have more than one possible source, and problems are cross-referenced in the briefs where appropriate. Read the brief or briefs that apply to your problem to find out where to start.

Following each troubleshooting brief, a section of *project data* will inform you about the special tools and materials you need, and about job time and difficulty. Some of the more commonly used troubleshooting tools include a compression gauge, hand-held vacuum pump, tachometer, and volt/ohmmeter, some of which you may already own. In general, buy tools only as you need them, and buy good-quality tools. Job times and difficulty evaluations are by nature subjective, but they should give you a sense of the relative skill and time needed for the tasks in the chapter.

Safety

Most important, the project data in this book feature vital safety precautions. Any machine presents potential hazards, and a machine as powerful as a car can hurt you whether it's in motion or at rest. Treat it with great respect in either case: *Always* follow scrupulously the safety precautions given. If there's a particular procedure you shouldn't attempt—because you lack professional expertise or an essential but costly tool—the book will warn you away from it. Read the safety precautions carefully and, when in doubt about your own ability to do a task safely, make the better judgment to err on the side of caution and let a mechanic do the work for you.

Before You Begin

Make sure you understand what you're doing—and why—*before* you start. Once you've identified the system that needs your attention and you've read the troubleshooting brief and project data, read the chapter through before attempting any work. Understanding the function of the system you're checking is the key to effective troubleshooting. Reading the entire chapter gives you that overall view.

If you plan ahead, take your time, and work carefully, the instructions in *What's Wrong with My Car?* can help you work like a pro to find the causes of aggravating and potentially costly performance problems. If you ever feel that a given procedure is "over your head," beyond your skill and comfort level, we urge you again to let a professional mechanic do the work. At the very least, you will be able to talk more knowledgeably with your mechanic about the problem and increase the likelihood that a satisfactory repair can be made.

1

Fuel Systems and Feedback Carburetors

TROUBLESHOOTING BRIEF

Many problems surface when a part of a car's fuel-delivery system malfunctions. They include hard starting, hesitation and stalling, rough idle, and poor gas mileage. A fault in the fuel-delivery system may also cause a fuel or fuel-vapor leak, resulting in a gasoline odor.

The fuel-delivery system consists of those parts between the gas cap and the carburetor that are involved in bringing gasoline into the engine: the fuel tank, fuel lines, fuel filter, and fuel pump. Technically part of the emissions control system, the charcoal canister and vapor-recovery lines are closely related to the fuel-delivery system and are included in this chapter. These parts are often called the fuel-evaporation control or vapor recovery system. A gasoline odor often accompanies failure of a fuel-evaporation control part. This chapter does not cover carburetor troubleshooting. Even the section in this chapter on feedback (electronic) carburetors centers on the system that allows this type of carburetor to work—not on the carburetor itself. If your car's performance problem is eventually traced to the carburetor, feedback or not, seek the services of a professional mechanic if you are not experienced with carburetor repair procedures and do not have the manufacturer's repair manual. Carburetors usually don't give trouble for the first 75,000 to 100,000 miles. Then, car owners usually discover that it is more economical to install a remanufactured unit than it is to repair the old carburetor.

The fuel-delivery system is another matter. Parts can malfunction at any time. Therefore, you will want to know how to inspect the fuel-delivery system to locate the cause of the trouble.

This chapter does not deal with electronic fuel injection systems.

PROJECT DATA

Special tools and materials. Manufacturer's repair manual, fuel-line wrench, safety ramps or safety stands, dry chemical (class B) fire extinguisher, portable gasoline holding-tank, vacuum/pressure gauge, vacuum pump, timing light, analog volt/ohmmeter.

Possible replacement parts. Gas cap, fuel filter, charcoal-canister filter or charcoal canister, fuel pump.

Tasks that require two people. Testing and replacing a fuel pump.

Job difficulty and time. Degree of difficulty is relative to the mechanic's experience; all times are approximate.

- Tightening fuel-line fittings: Easy, 10–20 minutes.
- Servicing the fuel filter: Depending upon type of filter, easy to moderately difficult, 15–45 minutes.
- Replacing the filter of a charcoal canister or the charcoal canister itself: Easy, 15–30 minutes.
- Testing the fuel pump: Moderately difficult, 30–45 minutes.
- Replacing the fuel pump: Moderately difficult, 30–45 minutes.
- Testing General Motors feedback system: Easy, 15–30 minutes.
- Testing Ford feedback system: Easy, 15–30 minutes.
- Testing Chrysler feedback system: Easy, 15–30 minutes.

Safety precautions. In dealing with the fuel system, safety cannot be overemphasized. Gasoline is extremely flammable and the vapors that it gives off are insidious and highly explosive. Carelessness can result in serious and even fatal injury. Always observe the following safety procedures:

- Never smoke or bring any device that can create sparks near the car.
- Work outdoors, not in a closed area.
- Keep the negative cable disconnected from the battery, unless specifically instructed otherwise. If you must crank or run the engine to perform a test, reconnect the negative cable, but disconnect it immediately after the test has been completed.
- Keep a dry chemical (class B) fire extinguisher nearby.
- If a metal fuel line has to be replaced, make sure the replacement is a *metal* line of equal quality. One specified by the manufacturer in your car's repair manual will qualify. If you have to replace a fuel hose, make certain it is marked "Fuel Resistant," or with an equivalent statement, to indicate that gasoline will not degrade the hose. Again, the part recommended by the manufacturer in the repair manual is the safest to use. <u>Caution</u>: Never replace a metal fuel line with a fuel hose.

Fuel Delivery

An inspection of components that handle fuel will often allow you to uncover the reason for hard starting, hesitation and stalling, rough idle, poor gas mileage, or a gasoline odor. As mentioned, these components are the fuel tank, fuel-delivery and vapor-recovery lines, fuel pump, fuel filter, and charcoal canister (see Figure 1-1).

The system delivers gasoline to the carburetor, where it combines with air to form a combustible mixture, which is then sent to the engine. The fuel tank—normally located on the underside of the car toward the rear—is a sealed container. The cap used with most fuel tanks has two valves, pressure relief and vacuum relief, to deal

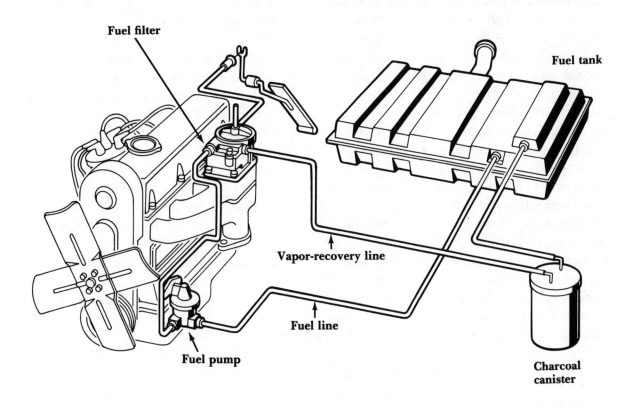

Fuel filter

Fuel tank

Vapor-recovery line

Fuel line

Fuel pump

Charcoal canister

Figure 1–1   Fuel-delivery and evaporation-control systems

with pressure build-up inside the tank or to equalize the difference when atmospheric pressure is greater than internal tank pressure. In the fuel tank of most cars with carburetors, the fuel line is attached to a fuel sender, which is a metering device that determines the rate of fuel flow. Fuel is pumped through the line to the carburetor by the fuel pump.

There are two types of fuel pumps, mechanical and electrical. Mechanical pumps are generally used in cars with carburetors; electric pumps are used in cars with electronic fuel injection. Both use the same principle of alternating vacuum and pressure to create a pumping action. The electric fuel pump has an advantage over mechanical types. It doesn't depend on the engine to operate, and can deliver fuel to the carburetor as soon as its circuit is completed.

Therefore, the engine is never starved for fuel.

The fuel-evaporation control system prevents fuel vapor from escaping into the atmosphere. The system incorporates the fuel tank and is sealed. Inside the tank, fuel vapor rises and travels through the vapor recovery line to the charcoal canister. When the engine is off, vapor from the carburetor float bowl also flows to the canister. Activated-charcoal particles in the canister absorb and hold the vapor. As the engine runs, vapor is drawn from the canister into the carburetor or intake manifold, where it mixes with air and enters the combustion cycle.

Begin a fuel-system inspection at the fuel tank by removing the gas cap and checking the cap's gasket. If part or all of the gasket is missing, you need a new cap.

Continue by inspecting the fuel tank and the fuel and vapor-recovery lines that run along the underside of the car. Disconnect the negative cable from the battery and lift the car using safety ramps, or by jacking and supporting the car on safety stands.

Caution: Raise a car only on firm, level ground. Using either safety stands or ramps, place an automatic transmission in Park or leave a manual transmission in gear and place chocks in front of the front wheels. If safety stands are used, lift the rear of the car high enough with a scissors jack to place stands under the left and right axle housings. Slowly lower the car until it is supported by the safety stands. If the stands shift, raise the car and reposition the stands. Do not try to support the rear of a car that has front-wheel drive with safety stands. Use safety ramps.

Look the tank over, making sure there are no leaks, dents, or rust. The straps that hold the tank to the car should be securely fastened to the body. Check the fuel-delivery line running from the tank to the fuel pump. Generally, this line is divided into three sections: (1) a flexible hose that goes from the tank to (2) a stainless-steel tube that is fastened to the chassis and extends to (3) another flexible hose that runs to the fuel pump.

Flexible hoses should be securely fastened at their ends, and there should be no leaks at the connecting points. If any part of the hose is cracked or leaking, replace the entire fuel line. Deterioration at one point signals existing or soon-to-exist deterioration elsewhere. Never try to tighten or loosen a fuel-line fitting with an open-end or adjustable wrench—you may damage the fitting. Use a fuel-line wrench.

Repair Tip: Replacing a fuel line involves removing the fuel tank from the car. The job should be done using a portable gasoline holding-tank that pumps gas from the tank and stores it safely. If you do not own or

have access to such a tank, leave the job to a professional mechanic.

Pay particular attention to the stainless-steel part of the fuel line. Make sure it is not dented. A dented line can reduce the flow of fuel to the carburetor and can cause the engine to hesitate, stall, and idle roughly.

Finally, be sure no part of the line is rubbing against any part of the car. Worn spots can develop tiny holes that allow gas to leak. A line rubbing against an adjacent part can also crack and let air into the system, which can affect the fuel mixture. The engine will then falter and stall.

Continue the inspection and examine the fuel pump (see Figure 1-2).

A mechanical fuel pump is driven by an eccentric lobe on the camshaft. When the diaphragm moves up, fuel is sucked from the fuel-tank line through an inlet valve into the pump. When the diaphragm moves down, fuel is forced out of the pump through the outlet valve. An electric pump uses an electromagnet to operate a flexible metal bellows. When the pump is energized, it pulls down the armature and extends the bellows. As the armature moves down, it opens contact points, cutting off current to the electromagnet. A return spring pushes up the armature, collapses the bellows, and forces fuel out. Then the contact points close and the cycle repeats itself.

Reconnect the battery's negative cable, start the engine, and observe the fuel pump. With a mechanical pump, if fuel comes out of the fuel-pump vent, which is the small air vent near the pump rocker arm, the pump's diaphragm is ruptured and the pump should be replaced (see page 10).

Shut off the engine and disconnect the battery's negative cable. Grasp the fuel pump and shake it to make sure it's mounted tightly. If it's loose, it can leak oil. Also, a loose pump will not supply the correct fuel volume and will wear out prema-

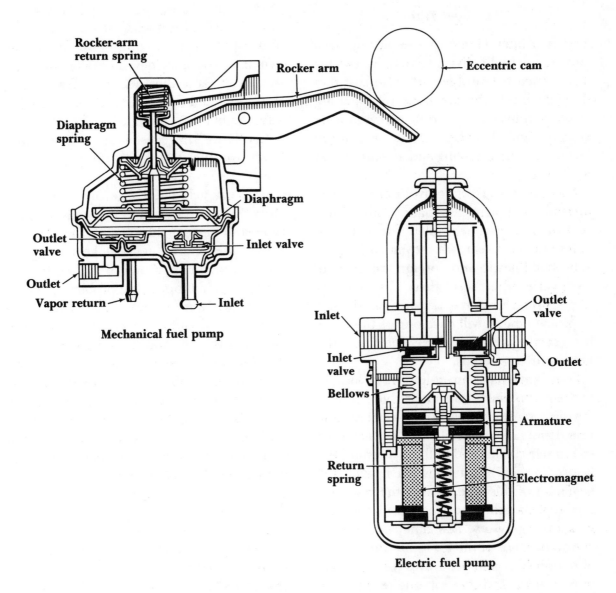

Figure 1–2   Mechanical and electric fuel pumps

turely. Damage to the lobe on the camshaft that moves the fuel-pump rocker arm is a possibility, too.

Repair Tip: If the lobe of the camshaft that works the fuel-pump rocker arm is damaged, the camshaft will have to be replaced. This is an extremely expensive repair. As an alternative to replacing the camshaft, you can install an electric fuel pump just outside the fuel tank. Electric pumps are available for practically every car

with an engine-mounted mechanical fuel pump. The old pump is removed and the hole in the block covered with a steel plate.

Look to see if the metal line that runs from the fuel pump to the carburetor is tight at both ends. If necessary use a fuel-line wrench to tighten connections. Hold the carburetor-inlet or fuel-pump-outlet nut securely with a second wrench (this can be open-end or adjustable) as you tighten (or loosen) a fuel-line fitting.

The Fuel Filter

The fuel filter is one of the more critical parts of the fuel-delivery system. It prevents dirt carried by gasoline, and also rust that develops inside the fuel tank, from getting to the carburetor and from there into the engine. Signs that the fuel filter is clogged include frequent stalling and an engine that has no power.

Maintenance Tip: To avoid engine performance problems associated with a dirty fuel filter, replace the filter every 15,000 miles or once a year, whichever comes first.

Both domestic and foreign car makers have varied the use of three types of fuel filters over the years. If your car doesn't have one type, it will have one of the other two. To replace a fuel filter, determine the kind your engine has.

Some cars have an in-line filter located between the fuel pump and carburetor that is visible on the fuel line between the fuel pump and carburetor. To replace it, cut off or remove clamps and pull the filter off. To insure proper filtration when installing a new filter of this type, be sure the arrow on the filter housing points toward the carburetor. Always use new clamps.

Another type of filter is located at the end of the fuel line and protrudes from the carburetor inlet. To replace it, unscrew the fuel line and turn the filter out of the carburetor with a wrench. A new filter needs only to be tightened up until it's snug. Some thread will remain exposed when the filter is correctly installed. This type of filter has a small flexible hose that connects it to the fuel supply line. Inspect this hose periodically. It tends to dry out and crack more quickly than other lines, because it's subjected to engine heat. If the hose is cracked, replace the filter.

A third type of filter fits inside the carburetor inlet and behind the inlet nut and out of sight. To replace it, unscrew the fuel line and then the fuel-inlet nut. The filter and a spring will pop out. Reuse the spring. When installing a new filter, be sure the open end faces the fuel line. If you place the closed end against the nut, fuel will bypass the filter.

Caution: After installing a new filter, check for fuel leaks with the engine running.

As a car gets older, the fuel tank often rusts. Rust particles can eventually clog the filter and restrict the flow of fuel. Therefore, if fuel filters you install keep clogging, have the fuel tank removed and cleaned at a tank-repair shop. If the problem persists, have a new tank installed. Avoid buying a tank from an auto wrecker; it could be as rusted as the one you're replacing.

Adulterated gasoline will also cause a fuel filter to clog. Furthermore, the dirt in adulterated fuel can damage the carburetor as well. You will then have to replace the carburetor.

Note: To assure yourself of getting clean, fresh gas, buy from name-brand stations located along heavily traveled roads.

Fuel-Evaporation Control

The final procedure involved in inspecting parts that handle gasoline is checking the charcoal canister and vapor hoses of the fuel-evaporation control system. Start by making sure hoses are properly routed to the charcoal canister. Consult the hose-routing decal in the engine compartment or check your manufacturer's repair manual to make sure hoses are properly connected.

Most canisters have a replaceable filter. If yours can be replaced, do this at the recommended interval given in the owner's manual. If you often drive under dusty conditions, change the filter more frequently.

Replacement is generally easy. Take off the canister by removing the screws or loosening the clamp that holds it. Pull the filter out of the base of the canister and install a new one. If the canister doesn't have a filter, install a new canister.

Gas Odors

A clogged charcoal canister or charcoal canister filter is a primary cause for an odor of gas inside the car or in the garage where you park the car. Obviously, another cause is a leaking fuel line or a damaged fuel evaporation emissions hose that allows fuel vapors to escape. Therefore, check all lines running to and from the fuel tank and use a fuel-line wrench to tighten or replace any that are leaking. Be sure to use the proper replacement line. A fuel evaporative-control system line (usually marked Evap) should be replaced only with an Evap line; a flexible fuel line only with one marked Fuel.

Another cause of gas odor around the car is a leaking fuel tank. If you smell gas, check the gas tank. You'll see a damp area on the tank or, if the leak is bad, on the ground. Although there are epoxies for repairing small gas-tank leaks, the best and safest procedure is to have a tank repair shop remove and replace the tank. Never try to weld, braze, or solder a fuel tank yourself; it's extremely dangerous. Repair shops purge the tanks of vapor before fixing them. Trying to repair one without purging it is like working on a bomb.

The Mechanical Fuel Pump

The fuel pump delivers gas from the fuel tank to the carburetor. If it has weakened, even slightly, the amount of gas the engine needs to run normally will be curtailed.

There are three checks to be made of the fuel pump: volume, pressure, and vacuum. A manufacturer's repair manual is needed to determine what the specifications are for the fuel pump in your car.

Volume To check fuel pump volume, remove the inlet line from the carburetor and attach a flexible hose over the end of it. Place the end of the hose in a calibrated glass or metal container.

Caution: Observe all safety measures given on page 4.

Have someone start the car and allow the engine to idle for 30 seconds (the engine will run for at least 30 seconds on the fuel in the carburetor float bowl). Then shut it off. Check the amount of fuel delivered to determine if that amount, about one pint in most cases, is in keeping with the amount specified in the repair manual.

Pressure To check fuel pump pressure, connect a vacuum/pressure gauge to the end of the fuel line. Make certain the gauge is securely attached to the end of the fuel line to prevent a gas leak and to assure an accurate test reading. Have someone start the engine and let it run for a few seconds until pressure stabilizes. The gauge should indicate the specified pressure for the engine as given in the repair manual. If you don't have specifications available, a rule of thumb regarding fuel pump pressure for most cars is 3 to 5 pounds per square inch (psi).

Vacuum If volume and pressure are within specifications, the fuel pump is in sound condition. If not, test fuel pump vacuum before deciding to replace the pump. A loss of vacuum resulting from a damaged fuel-tank to fuel-pump line may be causing low volume, low pressure, or both. The operation of the pump may be affected by damage to the fuel line, in which case replacing the fuel line could restore fuel-pump performance.

To check fuel-pump vacuum, use a fuel-line wrench to disconnect the fuel line from the gas tank at the fuel pump. Attach the vacuum/pressure gauge to the fuel-pump inlet and have someone in the car start the engine and let it run for a few seconds. The gauge should read what is specified in the repair manual, which will be 10 inches of mercury or more.

If the fuel pump operates at its vacuum specification, but you've gotten a low fuel pump pressure or volume reading, then there is probably a crack in the fuel line between the fuel tank and fuel pump. A crack will allow air to enter the system and prevent the pump from creating strong vacuum—vital if the pump is to do its job. Replace the fuel line or have it replaced by a professional mechanic (see page 6).

Suppose, however, the fuel pump vacuum test confirms that the fuel pump is faulty. The pump should be replaced. As the pump gets weaker and weaker, it will deliver less and less gas. In time, the hesitation and stalling problem the pump is causing will lead to hard starting as well.

Replacing a Mechanical Fuel Pump
Installing a new fuel pump requires that you follow the safety precautions listed on page 4. Be sure to disconnect the battery negative cable.

Start by unscrewing the fuel lines from the fuel pump with a fuel-line wrench. Remove the pump mounting bolts and pull the pump from the engine. Clean the mounting surface on the engine block.

Squirt some oil into the rocker-arm area to lubricate it. Then put some grease on the new fuel-pump gasket surface, to hold the gasket in place, and slide the new pump into position. Do *not* use gasket sealer to hold the gasket. In time, gasket sealer can cause the gasket to dry and crumble. If this happens, oil can be lost from the engine around the fuel-pump to engine joint.

If the pump won't go into place, reconnect the battery cable. First, ground the ignition coil high tension cable to keep the engine from starting, then have someone in

the car crank the engine until the eccentric lobe on the cam is in its low position. The pump should slide into place. (With General Motors cars equipped with high-energy-ignition [HEI], you'll have to disconnect the BAT terminal at the distributor, because the coil is located in the cap.)

General Motors' V8 engines have a push rod that goes between the cam's drive lobe and the fuel-pump rocker arm. To keep this from falling down as you install the pump, put some grease on the rod to hold it in place.

Now bolt the pump loosely in place and thread the fuel lines onto the pump finger-tight. Finish by tightening all lines. Be sure to use a fuel-line wrench.

Important: Change engine oil and filter when you replace the fuel pump since oil could have been contaminated by fuel leaking into the engine from the pump.

Feedback Carburetors

There are millions of cars now in use that have electronic control systems that monitor and regulate various engine processes. One of these processes, carburetion, is particularly tricky because to minimize emissions the carburetor should vaporize gasoline at a 14.7:1 air-to-fuel ratio. Even the most complex conventional carburetors lack the precision to meet strict emissions control standards. Therefore, the feedback carburetor was developed.

A feedback carburetor receives signals from various sensors via an electronic microprocessor (also called a computer) and provides a nearly perfect air-fuel mixture. But the electronically controlled carburetion is a technology that U.S. and foreign car manufacturers have approached differently. The operation details are unique to each system.

In general, you can troubleshoot a feedback carburetor if you can read a volt/ohmmeter, clip on jumper wires, and have patience. A manufacturer's repair manual for your particular car is essential. Without it, you'll be lost. In addition to the manual, you will need a hand-held vacuum pump, vacuum/pressure gauge, and timing light.

Basic Principles An interactive feedback-carburetor system works only during the "closed-loop" mode. *Closed loop* is a term that means sensors, computer, and carburetor are working with each other.

The electronic signal in a closed-loop system originates at an oxygen sensor that continually measures the oxygen content of the exhaust gases and converts the percentage of oxygen into an electrical signal. A lean, or oxygen-rich, mixture yields a low sensor output of about 0.1 or 0.2 volt. A rich, or oxygen-starved, mixture makes the sensor generate a higher voltage, with an upper limit of 0.6 to 0.8 volt. By measuring oxygen levels, the sensor indirectly measures the air-to-fuel ratio.

The electrical signal travels from the oxygen sensor to the control module, which is a small microprocessor with the ability to receive signals and send commands to various components based on information received (see Figure 1–3). During the closed-loop mode the microprocessor receives the oxygen sensor's signal along with similar signals from sensors that measure engine-coolant temperature, barometric pressure, intake manifold pressure, throttle position, and possibly other conditions. The microprocessor monitors all incoming information and calculates whether to enrich or lean out the air-fuel mixture. To make a change in mixture, the computer sends a signal to a solenoid or stepper motor on or inside the feedback carburetor.

All this occurs in the closed-loop mode. Under some conditions, such as cold starting, hot idling, and wide-open throttle, the system works in the "open-loop" mode, in which the microprocessor ignores signals from the oxygen sensor. Instead, it gives the carburetor a preprogrammed command for a slightly richer than average mixture.

Feedback-carburetor systems are simple in theory. All the complicated parts are in the computer, sensors, and carburetor. Servicing the systems requires testing to find the defective part.

When it comes to tracking down the reason for an engine performance problem, check the rest of the engine before doing anything to the feedback system. If the engine idles roughly, for instance, do a tune-up. Inspect all vacuum hoses and pay special attention to their ends, which can dry out and crack. A leaking or cracked vacuum hose is more likely to cause a performance problem than is a defective part of the feedback system.

Before testing sensors, pull apart electrical connectors of the electronic control system. Clean out any corrosion using a small brush or sandpaper and straighten bent terminal pins with needle-nose pliers. Check all grounds. Complete circuits are important to a feedback system because of the extremely low voltages involved. With only 0.2 volt tolerance, there's no excess voltage to lose at a loose or dirty connection.

To give you an idea of what to expect when you troubleshoot your feedback carburetor, a look at the three major U.S. automakers' systems follows. Each system requires a different procedure. The feedback carburetors of other makes of cars, whether manufactured here or abroad, operate under the same basic principles.

General Motors Talking Computer

The General Motors Computer Command Control (3C) system serves both the fuel and ignition systems. One of its advantages is its

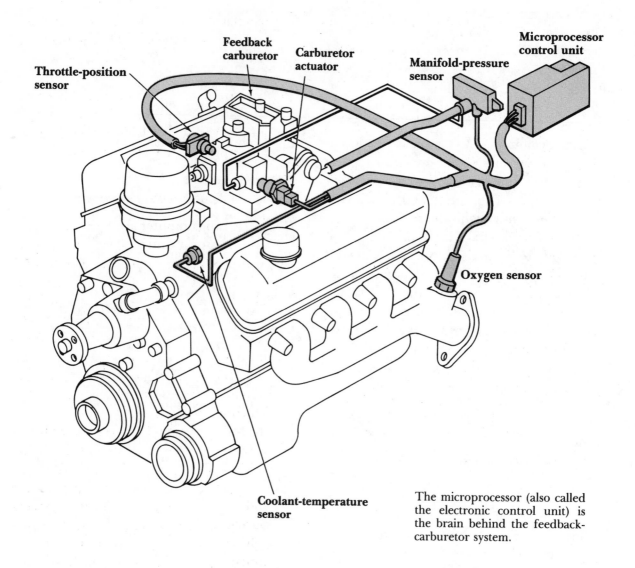

Throttle-position sensor

Feedback carburetor

Carburetor actuator

Manifold-pressure sensor

Microprocessor control unit

Oxygen sensor

Coolant-temperature sensor

The microprocessor (also called the electronic control unit) is the brain behind the feedback-carburetor system.

Figure 1–3 A simple feedback carburetor system

self-test capability. Once the self-test circuit is on, all you need to do is count the flashes of the Check Engine light on the dash. The flashes will indicate any one of thirteen problem code numbers, which can be deciphered using the repair manual.

If your car's Check Engine light comes on or the engine runs poorly, begin testing by activating the self-test circuit. To do that, you must first locate the computer. It's under the passenger-side dashboard in air-conditioned cars; behind the passenger-side

kick panel in others. Once you've found it, check over its wiring harness until you locate an unattached green connector hanging from a black-and-white wire. With the engine off, ground this lead using a jumper wire. Now, watch the Check Engine light. It should show a number 12 code by flashing once, pausing, then flashing twice in succession.

The number 12 code will flash unless other problems are detected or until the engine is started. This code means that there is no tachometer signal going to the computer, which makes sense since the engine is off. If the light does not flash, either the wiring or the microprocessor is bad. Every time you ground the test lead, check for a number 12 code; then you'll know the self-tester is working.

Now, disconnect the jumper and start the engine. Reconnect the wire and watch the light. It will flash one or more codes three times each.

Normally the microprocessor has short-term memory and will recall applicable trouble codes starting from when the ignition was last switched on. Once the ignition is turned off, however, short-term memory is erased. If a number 21 code flashes each time the ignition is turned on, for example, the repair manual will tell you there's something wrong with the throttle-position sensor circuit.

But perhaps you're trying to corner an elusive, intermittent problem indicated by a trouble code that sometimes flashes and sometimes doesn't. The module has the ability to remember for long periods, too.

To connect the long-term memory, a jumper wire must be run from the battery to the S terminal on the computer. A wire from the S terminal runs to a four-terminal connector that can be found under the dash, just to the left of center. There's one open space in the connector; this is where you clip your hot jumper wire. With battery power to the S terminal, long-term memory is actuated and turning the ignition off and on no longer causes the microprocessor to delete the problem codes. You can run the car—for days if necessary—until you're sure the intermittent problem has struck, then ground the green connector to get the flashing code.

Some cautions apply when making a long-term connection. First avoid disconnecting the battery. The memory will erase if power is terminated. Second, letting the car sit for long periods with the long-term memory actuated could result in a dead battery.

Using long-term memory may often be more convenient than running a short-term test, because some codes take up to eight minutes of running at 1,500 revolutions per minute (rpm) or more to complete.

Ford Feedback System

Ford has two computer systems: the simple Microprocessor Control Unit (MCU) and the complex Electronic Engine Control III (EEC III). EEC III is a high-tech, comprehensive system. The computer is connected to seven sensors and is housed in two boxes. It commands five systems besides the feedback carburetor. A self-test program is included, but it can't be run without the Electronic Engine Control System Tester, which costs over $1,500.

The MCU system which controls only air-fuel ratio and exhaust gas recirculation (EGR) is less comprehensive than EEC III, and you can tap into its diagnostic program to find out what's wrong with the feedback-carburetor system. Unlike the General Motors 3C system, you'll need an analog volt/ohmmeter to read it. An under-hood connector is provided for the negative volt/ohmmeter lead. The positive meter lead goes to the battery's positive post. A few vacuum connections and disconnections are necessary, the carburetor's fast-idle cam must be on its lowest setting, and the positive crankcase ventilation (PCV) valve must be removed. The fifteen codes are read on the 16-volt, DC scale as a series of voltage surges. A number 41 code (lean air-fuel ratio), for example, will show as four surges followed later by one surge. The first test is done with the engine off. A running test portion follows with up to twenty possible codes. Secondary checks of the pinpointed problems are then made, many with a volt/ohmmeter.

If the test code shows that the oxygen sensor is constantly giving rich signals, for example, you could narrow the cause down to a bad sensor, faulty sensor wiring, or malfunctioning carburetor actuator. Several voltage and ohm checks later you should know just where the problem is located by following the test sequence in the manufacturer's repair manual.

Chrysler Silent System

The Chrysler system (see Figure 1-4) is simpler than either General Motors' or Ford's, but no self-test feature is available. Chrysler's electronic oxygen-feedback solenoid works in conjunction with a conventional fixed main-metering jet in the carburetor. When power is off, the valve spring holds the valve open, allowing a rich fuel mixture. With power on, the valve is pushed down to close off the opening, giving the leanest fuel mix for any air flow. By controlling the time the power is on, the solenoid regulates

the fuel-air ratio between extremes. Some Chrysler feedback systems are operated by a vacuum regulator instead of by a solenoid in the carburetor. (The General Motors solenoid is connected to the carburetor's metering rods; the stepper motor that controls Ford carburetors has 120 positions and information going to the motor is updated ten times a second.)

All performance checks, which are detailed in the Chrysler repair manual, must be done with a volt/ohmmeter, vacuum pump, and other standard test and tune-up tools.

Chrysler has broken down the troubleshooting procedure into four categories: visual inspection, no-start, and cold-engine and warm-engine driveability. If, for example, your engine starts and warms up well, but stumbles when warm, then you need only follow the visual-inspection and warm-engine-driveability procedures.

An oxygen sensor test illustrates Chrysler's step-by-step method. The repair manual shows a green wire leading from the carburetor; you need to connect that wire

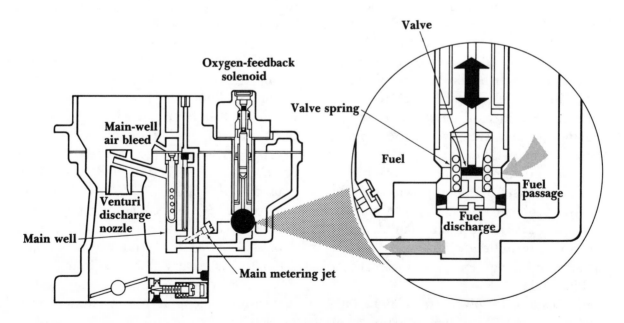

Figure 1–4   Chrysler electronic oxygen-feedback solenoid and carburetor

to a volt/ohmmeter. Instead of breaking a wiring connection to do so, use a fine needle or pin to pierce the wire's insulation (wrap the hole with electrical tape when you're done). Connect the volt/ohmmeter's positive lead to the pin; connect the other meter lead to a good ground. Start the engine and let it run at 2,000 rpm; hook up a tachometer or have an assistant press the accelerator about half way to the floor. Close the choke plate by hand and hold it down; within 10 seconds the volt/ohmmeter should read a steady three volts or less. If it doesn't, dis-connect the hose at the positive crankcase ventilation (PCV) valve. Voltage should rise to a steady nine volts or better. If it does, there may be a problem with the PCV system. If it doesn't, you'll have to replace the oxygen sensor.

Tests such as these make up feedback-carburetor troubleshooting. If you can find your way through a standard carburetor and have basic skills and the proper repair manual, you'll be able to check your electronically controlled carburetor.

2

Electronic Ignition

TROUBLESHOOTING BRIEF

When there is a failure of the electronic ignition (EI) system, the engine will be hard to start or won't start at all although it cranks briskly. If the engine does start, it may run roughly at idle and low speeds, or misfire at high speeds.

Since it is not possible to discuss in detail every variation of the electronic ignition system used by cars since 1971 (the year Chrysler Corporation introduced electronic ignition into passenger cars on a wide-ranging basis), this chapter relies on the Chrysler system to provide an example of how to troubleshoot a typical electronic ignition system. If you own a car not made by Chrysler, it is important that you review this chapter with a special attitude: First, there are similarities in troubleshooting between the Chrysler system and the systems used by other domestic and foreign manufacturers. You will want to note these. Second, if you find it easy to understand how the Chrysler system works, then you will better understand the system in your car. With one exception as noted, General Motors, the electronic ignition systems used by the various manufacturers are quite similar to Chrysler's. But you must have the manufacturer's repair manual for your car.

PROJECT DATA

Special tools and materials. Manufacturer's repair manual, screwdriver with insulated handle, insulated spark-plug cable pliers, volt/ohmmeter, plastic feeler gauge.

Possible replacement parts. Secondary circuit distributor to ignition-coil cable, spark-plug cables, distributor cap, rotor, dual ballast resistor, pickup coil, vacuum advance.

Tasks that require two people. Testing the overall performance of the ignition system with the spark intensity test.

Job difficulty and time. Degree of difficulty is relative to the mechanic's experience; all times are approximate.

- Spark intensity test: Easy, 10–15 minutes.
- Inspecting the distributor to ignition-coil cable and spark-plug cables: Easy, 30–45 minutes.
- Testing the primary circuit: Easy, 45–60 minutes.

Safety precautions. When you work on a car, the danger of explosion from fuel vapors always exists. Therefore, never smoke or bring a device that creates sparks near the car, always work outdoors (not in an enclosed space), and always keep a dry chemical (class B) fire extinguisher nearby.

- Beware of pulleys and belts when the engine is running; never wear loose clothing, watches, rings, or other jewelry when working on a car.
- Keep the negative cable of the battery disconnected except when making tests that require that the engine be cranked or the ignition switch be turned on. Disconnect the negative cable after completing such a test.
- When doing the spark intensity test, keep the sparking end of the spark-plug cable pointed toward a part of the engine that is as far away as possible from the carburetor, which exudes fuel vapors.
- Never hold a spark-plug cable in your hand while the engine is being cranked. You may get a shock. Hold the cable using insulated spark-plug cable pliers.
- With a spark-plug or the distributor-to-ignition-coil cable disconnected, crank the engine for no more than two seconds. Prolonged cranking may damage the catalytic converter.

Pinpointing Ignition Trouble

Not even the relatively reliable parts of an electronic ignition (EI) system can last forever. A spark intensity test will let you know at once whether failure to start is ignition-caused. <u>Note:</u> You can use this test to troubleshoot any EI system, not just Chrysler's.

1. Twist a spark-plug boot off a plug. The best way to remove spark-plug cables from plugs is with insulated spark-plug pliers (see Figure 2-1). Pull on the boot, not on the cable. Never use regular pliers.

2. Push a screwdriver or metal paper clip inside the boot so it makes contact with the cable terminal. (If you use a screwdriver, make sure it has an insulated handle.)

3. Grasp the boot with a pair of insulated spark-plug cable pliers or grab the insulated screwdriver handle. Hold the metal clip or screwdriver shank as far away from the carburetor as possible and ¼ inch away from a clean, dry metal part of the engine, such as an engine bolt.

4. Have someone in the car crank the engine, but for no more than two seconds.

If a bright blue spark jumps the gap, you do not have an ignition problem to deal

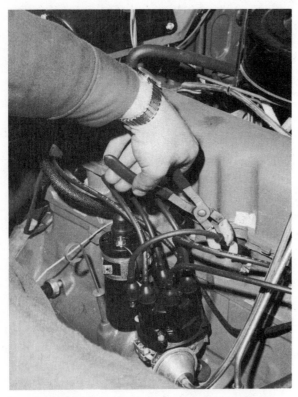

Figure 2–1   Using insulated spark-plug cable pliers to remove spark-plug cables

with. But if there is no spark or the spark is weak or yellow, there is a problem in the ignition system, located in either the secondary (high-voltage) circuit or the primary (low-voltage) circuit.

The ignition coil is part of both the primary and secondary ignition circuits. If the coil malfunctions, the engine will not start. Other than inspecting the coil for cracks or corroded electrical terminals, however, there's nothing a do-it-yourselfer can do to test a coil. Testing requires an oscilloscope or ignition-coil tester, which are expensive pieces of equipment. Moreover, if you find no cracks or corrosion, it's much more likely that another part of the ignition system is causing the problems. Perform the tests in the sections that follow. If you find no problems with any other ignition-system component, have the coil tested by a professional mechanic, and replace it if necessary.

The Secondary Circuit

Once you establish that the engine isn't starting because of an ignition problem, inspect the secondary ignition circuit first. The secondary circuit carries high voltage to the spark plugs. It consists of the high-voltage cable between the ignition coil and distributor cap, and the distributor cap, rotor, spark-plug cables, and spark plugs.

Spark-plug cables and spark plugs usually fail one at a time. Rather than not starting at all, an engine with a damaged cable or dead plug becomes hard to start and misses once it does start. A damaged high-voltage cable between the ignition coil and distributor cap, a cracked distributor cap, or a damaged rotor usually prevents the engine from starting.

<u>Note:</u> The following inspection procedure relative to an ignition system secondary circuit applies to all EI systems, not just Chrysler's.

Begin inspecting the secondary circuit by first making certain the high-voltage cable is securely connected to the ignition coil and to the center distributor tower (see Figure 2-2). Also, see that the two thinner (primary circuit) wires flanking the cable at the coil are tight. If the cable or one of the primary circuit wires is loose, the engine will not start or will be hard to start.

With all but General Motors vehicles, remove the high-voltage cable between the coil and distributor and test it using a volt/ohmmeter. The cable should show a resistance of no more than 25,000 ohms. If it shows more, replace it. (General Motors uses a High Energy Ignition [HEI] system in which the ignition coil is housed inside the distributor cap and several wires attached to the cap handle current. Make sure all wires and cables attached to the HEI distributor are secure.)

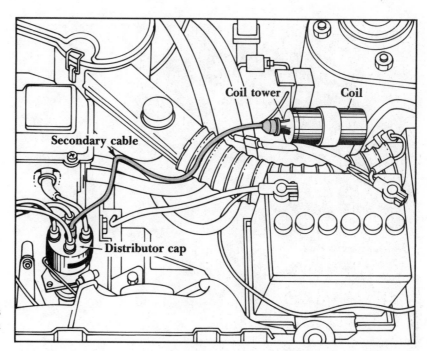

Figure 2–2 The secondary cable runs between the ignition coil and distributor cap

This key ignition-system part is often overlooked when ignition failure occurs.

Also, test the resistance of all spark-plug cables. Again, a reading of more than 25,000 ohms is reason for replacing a cable.

Remove each spark plug and examine the electrodes for oil sludge and carbon deposits. Oil-fouled plugs indicate that too much oil is entering the cylinder, which is a symptom of serious engine problems such as worn pistons or rings, or worn valve stems, valve-stem seals, or valve guides. Have a professional mechanic determine the cause. A dirty air filter, defective fuel pump, overly rich fuel mixture, or malfunctioning heat riser valve can cause carbon to build up on the electrodes of a spark plug. If you can't pinpoint the reason for the buildup, have a professional mechanic find the cause and make repairs. Replace the plugs. Also, to ensure that worn plugs won't create ignition problems, replace spark plugs at the intervals recommended in the owner's manual.

Resume your check of secondary circuit components by taking off the distributor cap and rotor. Examine both for cracks, burned or corroded terminals, and carbon tracks (see Figure 2-3). A carbon track is a trace of carbon that indicates a hairline crack in the cap or rotor. If the distributor cap or rotor shows a visible crack or a carbon track, replace it.

The Primary Circuit

If you can't find the reason for ignition failure by testing secondary circuit components, turn your attention to the primary circuit. The primary circuit steps up the low voltage supplied by the battery (about 12 volts) to the high voltage needed by spark plugs to ignite the fuel mixture. High voltage developed by a properly functioning electronic ignition system can reach 50,000 volts.

In the Chrysler electronic ignition system, the primary circuit consists of a ballast resistor, electronic control unit (ECU), reluctor, pickup coil, and wiring between these units. The reluctor and pickup coil are inside the distributor. All other parts are external and visible.

The following step-by-step procedure can help you uncover a defect that exists in the

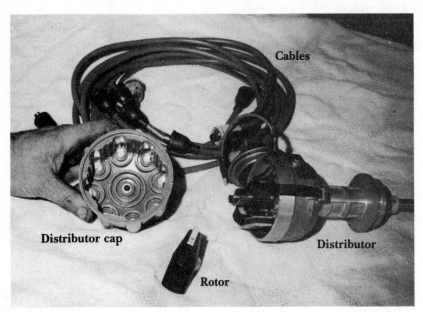

Figure 2–3 Distributor cap, rotor, and distributor with spark-plug cables

Since they handle high voltage, the distributor cap and rotor are more likely to go bad than parts of the ignition system that handle low voltage.

primary circuit of a Chrysler EI system. Similar techniques can be used to uncover problems in the EI systems of other makes of cars; check the manufacturer's repair manual for details.

The Battery Since current for the ignition system begins at the battery, test the battery by connecting a voltmeter between the battery positive terminal and ground. Crank the engine. The voltmeter should record at least 9.6 volts. If the reading is lower than this, charge the battery and retest it. If the problem persists, test the charging and starting systems (see chapter 3).

Wire Connections With the ignition switch off, disconnect the multiwire connector from the plug of the ECU (see Figure 2-4). Caution: The bright metal button in the ECU near the multiwire connector is the power-switching transistor. It handles high

Figure 2–4 The electronic control unit, power-switching transistor, and ECU multiwire connector

With a Chrysler electronic-ignition system, the electronic control unit is normally bolted to the engine firewall or fender liner. The pointer in the photograph is aimed at the power-switching transistor, which presents a severe shock hazard when the ignition is on. The multiwire connector that must be disconnected when doing tests is just to the left of the pointer.

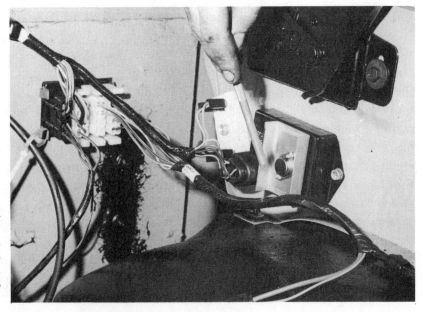

voltage when the ignition is on. *Do not touch it.* Doing so when the ignition is on may result in a severe shock.

With the ignition still switched off, connect the positive lead of a voltmeter to cavity number 1 of the multiwire connector and the negative lead of the voltmeter to ground (see Figure 2-5). Turn the ignition switch on.

The voltmeter should read battery voltage plus or minus 1 volt. If the reading falls outside this range, inspect the wiring connections between the ballast resistor, ignition switch, alternator warning light (or gauge), and battery. They should be clean and tight.

Repeat the same test for cavities number 2 and number 3 of the multiwire connector (Figure 2-5). (Note that the number 3 cavity and pin are omitted from most Chrysler EI systems of 1980 and newer models. See page 22.) Caution: Turn off the ignition switch when connecting the voltmeter, then turn it on to make the test. Normal test readings are equal to the voltage reading you got when you tested the battery, plus or minus 1 volt. If you don't get this reading, inspect all wiring connections.

The Dual Ballast Resistor   If when testing cavity number 1 you get a voltmeter reading that isn't normal, but wire connections are clean and tight, the dual ballast resistor may be defective. As the name implies, the dual ballast resistor is two resistors in one. One side of the unit is called the *compensating side.* The compensating side of the dual ballast resistor maintains primary current at a constant level although engine speed varies. When the engine is cranked, current bypasses this part of the ballast resistor so that full battery voltage can be applied to the ignition coil. In 1980 and newer models, the compensating side is a 1.2-ohm resistor. In pre-1980 models, the compensating side of the ballast resistor is a 0.5-ohm resistor.

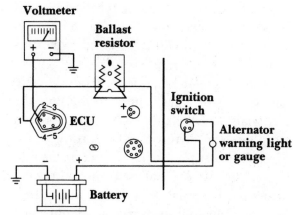

A. Voltmeter hookup for cavity number 1

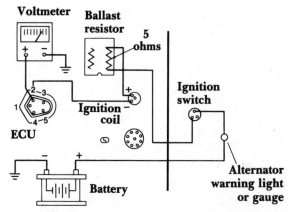

B. Voltmeter hookup for cavity number 2

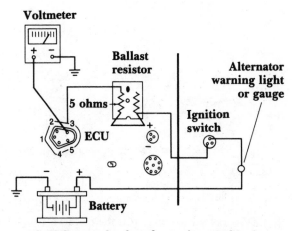

C. Voltmeter hookup for cavity number 3

Figure 2–5   Ignition-switch wiring

The other side of the dual ballast resistor is called the auxiliary side. This 5-ohm resistor protects the ECU from excessive current.

Before disconnecting wires from the dual ballast resistor, mark them to identify the terminals to which they connect. You can wrap tapes of different colors around each wire. Then use grease pencils to note matching colors on the ballast-resistor housing near each terminal. Mark wires and terminals carefully to prevent reconnecting wires incorrectly, which may damage EI components.

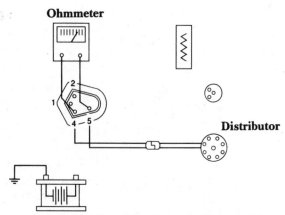

A. Ohmmeter hookup to test the pickup coil in pre-1980 cars

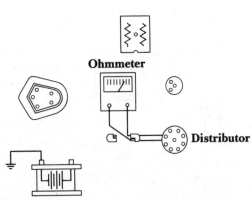

B. Ohmmeter hookup to test the connector that joins the distributor to the multiwire connector

Figure 2–6   Pickup-coil and distributor wiring

Caution: Keep the ignition switch off during this test.

Connect an ohmmeter across the two top terminals of the ballast resistor. Record the reading. Then, connect the ohmmeter across the two bottom terminals. Record the reading.

With the ohmmeter connected one way, you should get a resistance reading of 1.2 to 1.3 ohms or 0.5 to 0.6 ohm, depending on the year of the car. This is the resistance of the compensating side of the dual ballast resistor. With the ohmmeter connected the other way, you should get a reading of 4.75 to 5.75 ohms. This is the resistance of the auxiliary side of the ballast resistor.

If either of the readings is not within specification, replace the ballast resistor by unscrewing the faulty unit from its mounting and screwing on a new unit.

Caution: Make sure the negative cable of the battery is disconnected when you replace the dual ballast resistor.

The Pickup Coil With the ignition switch off, connect an ohmmeter between the cavities numbered 4 and 5 of the multiwire connector (see Figure 2-6). You should get a reading of 150 to 900 ohms. If you don't, pull apart the connector that joins the distributor and multiwire connector. Attach an ohmmeter to the part of the connector on the distributor side (see Figure 2-6). Keep the ignition switch off.

If the ohmmeter gives a reading of 150 to 900 ohms, reconnect the two parts of the connector tightly. A loose connector may be the cause of your problem. But if the ohmmeter reading still doesn't fall between 150 and 900 ohms, unscrew the pickup coil from its seat in the distributor, install a new one, and set the gap between the pickup coil and reluctor (see "Inside the Distributor" below).

The Electronic Control Unit If the cause of trouble still hasn't been found, turn your attention to the multiwire connector pins and the ECU. Identify the pin coinciding with multiwire connector cavity number 5. With the ignition switch off, hook one lead of an ohmmeter to connecting pin 5 and the other lead to ground (see Figure 2-7).

If the ohmmeter shows other than zero ohms, make certain the battery negative cable is disconnected and remove the electronic control unit. Use a wire brush to clean the back of the ECU and the ECU mounting area. Reattach the ECU, making sure bolts are tight. Do the test again. If this procedure results in an ohmmeter reading other than zero ohms, replace the ECU and dual ballast resistor as described in the repair manual.

Note: Since the ballast resistor protects the ECU, ECU failure may indicate that the ballast resistor has failed. Therefore, you should always replace the dual ballast resistor when replacing the ECU.

Inside the Distributor If the cause of ignition failure has still not revealed itself, remove the volt/ohmmeter and reconnect the multiwire connector securely to the ECU. Remove the distributor cap, which is held either by two retaining clips that you can snap loose with a screwdriver or by two screws. Then remove the rotor and adjust the gap between a reluctor tooth and pickup coil tooth as follows:

1. Engage the large nut of the crankshaft pulley with a wrench and turn the pulley clockwise until a reluctor tooth and pickup coil tooth line up.

2. Loosen the pickup coil adjusting screw and insert a plastic (nonmagnetic) feeler gauge between the reluctor tooth and pickup coil tooth. In most Chrysler cars, a 0.008-inch feeler gauge is required. However, for 1978 and 1980 models use a 0.006-inch feeler gauge.

3. Move the pickup coil in or out until a

This test shows whether the electronic control unit is causing ignition failure.

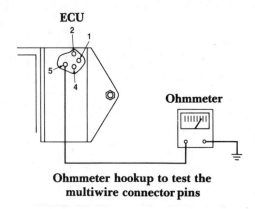

Ohmmeter hookup to test the multiwire connector pins

Figure 2–7   Electronic-control wiring

tooth of the pickup coil, feeler gauge, and a tooth of the reluctor come in contact. All three elements—pickup coil tooth, reluctor tooth, and feeler gauge—should touch, but you should be able to move the feeler gauge without having to use force. Tighten the pickup coil and adjustment screw.

4. Doublecheck the gap by trying to insert a larger size feeler gauge between the reluctor and pickup coil. Use a gauge 0.002 inch larger than the one you used to make the adjustment. You should not be able to get this gauge between the two teeth. If you can, the adjustment isn't correct, so you must repeat the procedure.

Vacuum Advance Disconnect the vacuum advance hose from the engine and suck on it or use a hand-vacuum pump to create a vacuum. Watch the pickup coil plate. It should rotate. If the pickup coil plate does not rotate as vacuum is applied, the vacuum advance unit is broken. Replace it; the repair manual outlines the procedure.

No pickup coil tooth should strike any tooth of the reluctor. If it does, the gap between the pickup coil and reluctor isn't set properly. Readjust the gap as described earlier.

3

The Battery and Charging System

TROUBLESHOOTING BRIEF

When a starting system cannot crank a car's engine powerfully enough to start it, the problem can usually be traced to the battery, alternator, or voltage regulator, or to the electrical wiring that connects these parts.

The battery provides electrical power for the starter motor when you turn the ignition switch. The starter motor gear engages the engine flywheel to crank and start the engine. The battery expends a great deal of energy each time it powers the starter motor. The alternator and voltage regulator, which are referred to as the charging system, provide current that restores the battery to full charge after it has used its energy to run the starter motor.

PROJECT DATA

Special tools and materials. Manufacturer's repair manual, battery charger, hydrometer, carbon-pile load tester (optional), voltammeter (often sold as an integrated tester, but can be purchased as separate instruments), 12-volt test lamp, battery-terminal puller, battery post- and terminal-cleaning brush, belt-tension gauge.

Possible replacement parts. Battery, battery cables, alternator drive belt, alternator, regulator.

Tasks that require two people. Battery load test using a voltammeter.

Job difficulty and time. Degree of difficulty is relative to the mechanic's experience; all times are approximate.

- Charging a battery: Easy, 60 minutes to several hours depending on how depleted the battery is.
- Testing battery state of charge: Easy, a few seconds to 10 minutes depending on whether the battery is maintenance-free or not.
- Testing the ability of a battery to hold a charge: Easy, 10–15 minutes.
- Checking for a short circuit: Easy, 10–15 minutes.
- Cleaning and tightening battery terminals: Easy, 15–30 minutes.
- Replacing and/or adjusting the alternator drive belt: Easy to moderately difficult, 15–30 minutes depending upon the complexity of the belt arrangement in the vehicle.
- Testing the charging system: Easy to moderately difficult, 5–15 minutes.
- Replacing the alternator and regulator: Moderately difficult, 30–45 minutes.

Safety precautions. Fuel in, and fuel vapors from, the fuel system and carburetor and the hydrogen given off by car batteries ignite easily and are highly explosive. When working on a car, never smoke or bring an open flame or device that creates sparks near the car. Work outdoors, not in an enclosed space, and always keep a dry chemical (class B) fire extinguisher nearby.

- Beware of pulleys and belts when the engine is running; never wear loose clothing, watches, rings, or other jewelry when working on a car.
- Always wear safety goggles and rubber gloves when handling or testing a battery. If battery acid should get on your skin, flush the area with cool water for at least 5 minutes. Consult a physician at once if battery acid gets in your eyes.
- Be sure to disconnect and connect battery cables from the battery correctly to avoid creating sparks near the battery. Use a battery-terminal puller to disconnect battery cables, and always disconnect the negative cable first. To reconnect battery cables, always connect the positive cable first.

The Battery

The battery provides a surge of high current to get the starter motor to engage, crank, and start the engine. Once the engine is running, the charging system takes over to supply electric current and to replenish the energy exhausted by the battery in powering the starter motor. If the battery doesn't get replenishment, it will lose all its charge during subsequent engine starts.

Battery Charging The battery should be charged before any tests are done on it. But first you must check the built-in indicator of a maintenance-free battery or perform a hydrometer test on a regular battery to make certain the battery has no cells with short circuits.

Caution: Wear safety goggles and rubber gloves. Never try to charge or jump start a battery with a shorted cell. The buildup of hydrogen gas created by charging a battery that has a short circuit could cause the battery to explode.

Most maintenance-free batteries have a built-in indicator that shows the state of charge by color. Green shows the battery is charged and working well. Black means the battery needs recharging. Yellow indicates that the battery has developed a shorted cell and must be replaced as soon as possible. A battery with a shorted cell will soon fail, if it hasn't already done so.

Use a hydrometer to test a battery that has removable vent caps. Each cell should read 1.240 (specific gravity points) or better. If the readings are less than 1.240, but all cells give even readings, you can charge the battery. A difference of 0.50 points or more between any two cells means the battery has developed a short circuit and must be replaced.

If the battery has no shorted cells, remove it and hook it up to a battery charger. If you don't own a battery charger, you'll have to bring the battery to a service station for recharging. Caution: Remove the vent caps of a regular battery before charging it; make sure the vent holes of a maintenance-free battery are not plugged. Battery posts are more fragile than they look and can be easily damaged. Never pry or twist off a cable; use a battery-terminal puller to prevent damage.

After the battery has been connected to the charger for an hour or so, check to make sure it is accepting the charge. If the indicator of a maintenance-free battery still shows black or if the cells of a regular battery give even readings of less than 1.240, continue the charging procedure for another two or three hours—but don't charge the battery longer than the manufacturer recommends. If at the end of that time the battery still has not accepted a charge sufficient to get the engine to start promptly, it cannot provide adequate power and will soon fail. Replace the battery.

Battery Testing   If the battery accepts a charge, you must next determine how well it holds a charge. The most accurate way to find out is to connect a carbon-pile load tester across the battery terminals. If you don't own or have access to a carbon-pile load tester, have the test done at a service station or garage.

A carbon-pile load tester is a heavy-duty variable resistor that simulates a steady load on the battery. It's adjusted to draw three times the battery's ampere-per-hour rating for 15 seconds. The ampere-per-hour rating for your battery may be printed on the battery. If it isn't, the owner or service manual will have it. The battery voltage during the test should not drop below 9.5 volts. If it does, the battery is almost worn out and should be replaced.

If you don't have access to a carbon-pile tester, you can get some indication of whether a battery is holding a charge by connecting a voltammeter across the battery terminals and cranking the engine (see Figure 3-1). Disconnect the secondary cable between the ignition coil and the distributor cap so the engine won't start. If your car is a GM model with the High Energy Ignition (HEI) system, disconnect the "B" or BAT wire at the distributor. Turn on the headlights to simulate a load and crank the engine for 15 seconds. If the voltammeter needle falls below 9.5 volts while the engine is cranked, the battery should be recharged and tested. If the battery fails the test again, replace it.

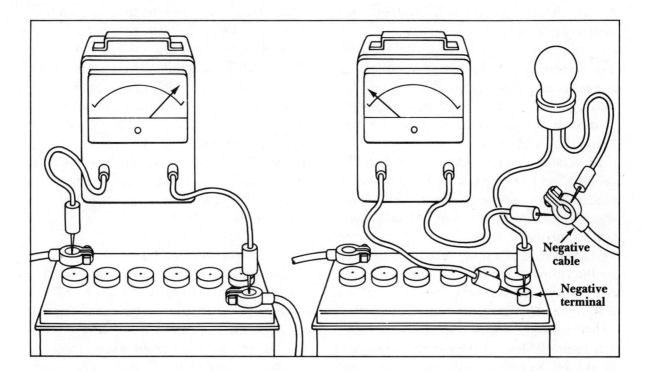

Figure 3–1   Battery load testing with a voltmeter

Figure 3–2   Testing for a short circuit with either an ammeter or a test lamp

Important: Be sure the battery is charged before performing a load test; otherwise, even a perfectly good unit will fail the test.

Short Circuits   Sometimes a battery accepts a charge and passes the load test, but seems to lose energy every couple of weeks and must be recharged because the engine fails to crank. In that case, a short in an electrical circuit may be draining energy from the battery. It doesn't take much current draw, as it's called, to run a battery down.

A quick and accurate way to check for a short is to remove the negative battery cable and connect one ammeter lead to the terminal end of the cable and the other to the battery post or terminal (see Figure 3-2). If you don't have an ammeter, connect a 12-volt test lamp in the same way. To make certain the ammeter or test lamp is con-

nected properly, turn on the headlights. As long as ammeter or test-lamp connections are secure, the ammeter needle will rise or the test lamp will glow.

Turn the headlights off, and check that all other accessories and the ignition switch are off. If you have a digital clock or any digital instruments, remove their fuses. Your owner's or repair manual shows the location of the fuse panel and the specific fuses that serve these devices. With all components that use electricity turned off, there should be no current draw; the ammeter needle should stay on zero or the test lamp should not glow or flicker. If the ammeter or test lamp acts to the contrary, there is a short circuit. You must now find the short's location.

You can isolate the circuit with the short by removing one fuse at a time from the fuse box. Once you have found the fuse that makes the current draw drop to zero, you'll have to check every electrical accessory and out-of-the-way light bulb in that circuit. If disconnecting a particular accessory or removing a bulb causes the ammeter to drop to zero or the test lamp to go out, you've found the trouble spot.

For example, remove the trunk light bulb. If this eliminates the drain, the trunk light bulb switch or socket is the culprit. Also, check engine- and glove-compartment lights. Move on to the fuse panel and remove one fuse at a time until the ammeter needle drops to zero or the test lamp goes out, thus pinpointing the troublesome circuit. Have an electrical specialist or professional mechanic test the circuit for you.

Battery Cables   If the battery is in good shape and no short circuits exist, check the battery cables next. Connections must be clean and tight. Inspect connections at each end of both cables. Many sound batteries and starter motors have been replaced because of damaged, corroded, or loose connections that prevented the flow of current.

First, examine cables for cracks in insulation. If a cable is damaged, replace it. Then, use a battery-cable puller to remove cables from battery posts, and clean terminals and battery posts with a terminal-cleaning brush (a two-in-one tool).

Caution: Wear safety goggles and rubber gloves.

If you've reached this point without having found out why the battery discharges periodically and can't provide energy to crank the engine, only one reason remains: The charging system is inadequate and is not charging the battery.

The Charging System

The alternator generates the electrical current necessary to charge the battery and power electrical components when the engine is running. The voltage regulator controls the amount of current the alternator produces. If unregulated, the amount of current produced by the alternator would damage electrical components and the battery.

Often, conditions that you can see, hear, and smell will tip you off to the existence of trouble with the alternator or regulator (see table). The following are the most common:

- alternator warning lamp on the instrument panel glows or gauge shows a negative reading
- headlights alternately flare and dim
- light bulbs burn out frequently
- alternator emits a loud whine or rattle that is heard above normal engine noise
- battery emits a rotten-egg odor

But a malfunctioning alternator or voltage regulator does not always send one of these signals. For example, a loose alternator drive belt is one of the most common reasons for a charging system to fail to produce enough current. Yet a loose belt may not give any one of the above warnings.

Drive Belts   An alternator and voltage regulator are reliable components that often give trouble-free service for a car's lifetime. If a reduction in current is apparent, check the alternator drive belt first. It is far more likely to be the reason for trouble than a defective alternator or regulator. A loose alternator drive belt can reduce the current output of the alternator significantly and cause the battery to run down. Belt tension, therefore, should be checked frequently.

One simple method is to place a straight edge across the pulleys and measure how much the belt deflects when you press firmly down on it midway between the pulleys. If the belt deflects more than ½ inch, tighten

Summary of Battery and Charging System Problems

Problem	Indication
Battery has no charge	The dashboard Alt (alternator) lamp is on or the alternator gauge shows zero or a slightly negative (−) reading.
Battery is discharging	The dashboard Alt lamp is lit or the alternator gauge shows a heavy discharge (−) reading, even with all electrical accessories off.
Battery is undercharged	The dashboard Alt lamp may occasionally glow dimly, or the alternator gauge shows a less-than-normal charge. The needle may point to the negative (−) side of the gauge when accessories are on.

The battery may slowly get weak and turn the starter more slowly than normal. Lights are dim. |
| Battery is overcharged | The Alt lamp is off, or the alternator gauge shows a higher-than-normal charge, even with all lights and accessories on. The battery uses water constantly. Lights are very bright, and bulbs and fuses may burn out rapidly. The battery gives off a rotten-egg odor. |
| Mechanical noises | Electrical system mechanical noises are sensitive to engine speed and are usually caused by a bad bearing in the alternator. |

it. A more accurate way to test belt tension is with a belt-tension gauge (see Figure 3-3). After checking tension, check both sides of the belt for damage. Replace a belt that is cracked or shiny.

Alternator Output When the battery keeps draining and the reason has not been found with the battery itself, the battery cables, a short circuit, or the alternator drive belt, perform an alternator-output test. This test measures the amount of current the alternator sends to the battery.

Connect a voltammeter to the battery positive terminal and to a ground. A properly functioning charging system will transmit 13 to 15 volts with the engine running at 1,500 rpm. If it doesn't, look for causes.

A shorted diode inside the alternator often causes alternator malfunction. Another cause is a shorted or open stator. One way to find these problems is with a "yes-no" charging-system tester that uses liquid emitting diode (LED) lamps. When this instrument is connected to the alternator field

Figure 3–3 Using a belt-tension gauge

as detailed in the repair manual or in the instructions that come with the tester, the unit will indicate if there is a shorted diode or a damaged stator. A green light indicates that all is well; a yellow light suggests a marginal condition; a red light warns of a breakdown. Connected to the battery terminal ("B" or BAT) of the alternator, the tester will also detect a bad battery or regulator.

If you do not have a charging-system tester and the alternator output test shows that the alternator is not maintaining the specified voltage, the charging system can be tested by doing a full-field test. This test is done by bypassing the regulator, as described below, so the regulator has no control over the alternator. In this way, you can determine whether the fault for an inadequate charge lies with the alternator or the regulator.

Many charging systems have the alternator and regulator as two separate units. To full-field test this system, the external regulator must be disconnected from the alternator and a jumper wire installed between the alternator field wire and, depending upon the car, the battery connection ("B" or BAT) or ground (see Figure 3-4). If you are full-field testing a system such as the GM Delcotron that has a voltage regulator inside the alternator, insert a small screwdriver into the D-shaped hole in the alternator housing to take the regulator out of service (Figure 3-4).

An alternator that's in good condition will show a high charging rate when full-field tested with the engine running at a high idling speed. A high charging rate is within 10 percent of the alternator's rated capacity as given in the repair manual. A defective alternator will show a lower rate or no charge at all.

If the alternator is sound, then the reason that the charging system has failed the alternator-output test lies with the voltage regulator. The repair manual describes how to make the replacements.

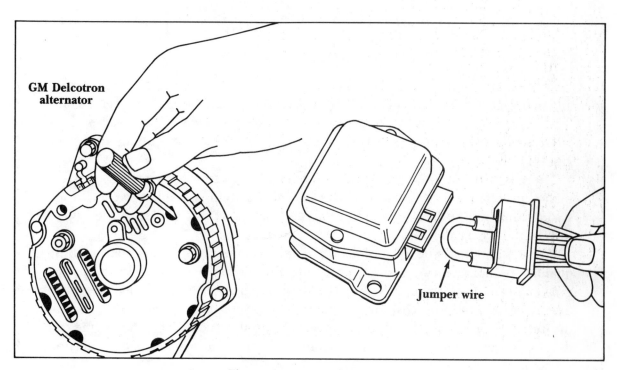

GM Delcotron alternator

Jumper wire

Figure 3—4   Full-field test

4

Emissions-Control Systems

TROUBLESHOOTING BRIEF

A car's engine can have as many as 17 parts that control emissions. Most car owners and many mechanics are not familiar with all of them, yet malfunctioning emissions-control parts are responsible for many performance problems. Among other problems, they can cause hard starting, detonation, hesitation and stalling, and poor gas mileage.

There is only one way to determine if emissions controls are causing a performance problem and, if so, which part of which system is to blame: check each system until you find the system at fault, and then check each part in the system until you discover the culprit.

There is another issue to consider when an emissions-control part goes bad: the quantity of noxious fumes discharged into the atmosphere. That issue has far greater importance than a hitch in vehicle performance. Not only is it illegal to disconnect an emissions control system, but doing so can cause serious damage to the engine. For example, if you disconnect the catalytic converter, the engine can develop a preignition condition (see chapter 6) that can cause damage to connecting rods and pistons.

Some cars equipped with electronic fuel injection do not possess an exhaust-gas-recirculation (EGR) system (refer to the manufacturer's repair manual for your car).

PROJECT DATA

Special tools and materials. Manufacturer's repair manual, carburetor-and-choke cleaner, hand-held vacuum pump, 12-volt test lamp, volt/ohmmeter.

Possible replacement parts. Positive-crankcase-ventilation (PCV) valve, filter, and hoses; carburetor air-cleaner filter; EGR valve and hose; thermostatic air cleaner ducts, hoses, vacuum motor, and temperature sensor; fuel-evaporation control system hoses, canister filter, and canister; idle-stop solenoid; electric-choke element; choke vacuum-break.

Tasks that require two people. Testing the EGR system; testing the electric choke and choke vacuum-break.

Job difficulty and time. Degree of difficulty is relative to the mechanic's experience; all times are approximate.

- Testing the PCV system: Easy, 15–30 minutes.
- Testing the EGR system: Easy to moderately difficult, depending on the type of EGR valve, 10–30 minutes.
- Testing the thermostatic air cleaner system: Easy, 20 minutes.
- Testing the fuel-evaporation control system: Easy, 15–30 minutes.
- Testing the idle-stop solenoid: Easy, 5–10 minutes.
- Testing the choke and choke vacuum-break: Easy, 10–20 minutes.

Safety precautions. Always bear in mind that fuel and fuel vapors from the fuel-delivery system and carburetor and hydrogen gas, which is given off by car batteries, ignite easily and are highly explosive.

- When working on a car, never smoke or bring a device that creates sparks near the car. Work outdoors, not in an enclosed space, and always keep a dry chemical (class B) fire extinguisher nearby.
- Watch out for pulleys and belts when the engine is running; never wear loose clothing, watches, rings, or other jewelry when working on a car.
- Wear heavy work gloves when doing tests that may bring your hands in contact with a hot engine.

Key Emissions-Control Systems

Carmakers have waged information campaigns urging professional mechanics to test emissions-control parts before doing expensive repairs such as replacing carburetors and ignition system components. Many experts believe that if mechanics would make certain that thermostatic air cleaners and exhaust-gas-recirculation valves, to name only two of these parts, are working before doing tune-ups, they would almost certainly contribute to a more healthful environment and resolve innumerable spark knock (detonation), stalling, and hesitation complaints—and save themselves time, and save their customers money.

Your car probably has many of the following emission controls (see Figure 4-1): positive crankcase ventilation (PCV), exhaust gas recirculation (EGR), thermostatic air cleaner, and fuel-evaporation control systems. A manufacturer's repair manual is needed to locate where the parts of these systems are in your car's engine compartment.

Positive Crankcase Ventilation

The PCV system draws combustion gases that accumulate in the crankcase into the engine, where they are burned (see Figure 4-2). PCV was the first emissions-control sys-

When an engine performance problem develops, its cause often lies with one of these parts.

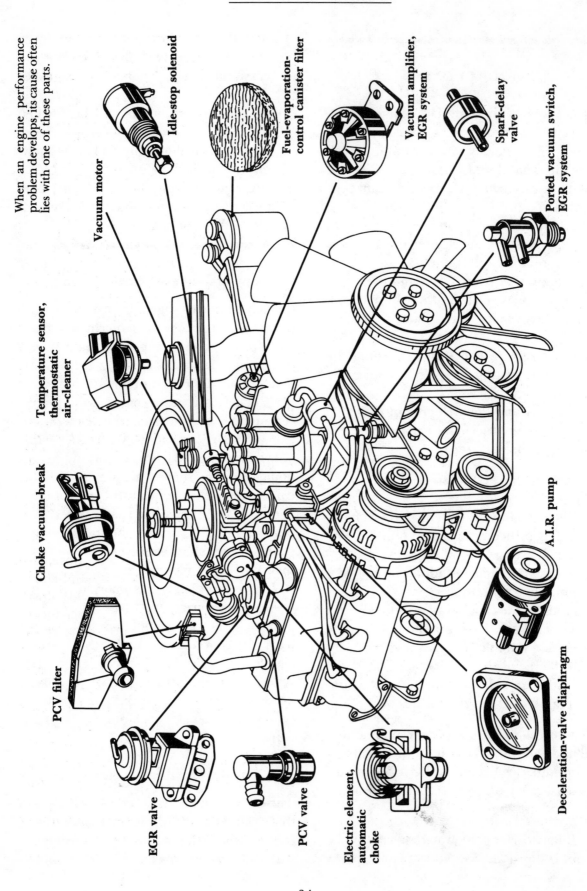

Vacuum motor

Idle-stop solenoid

Fuel-evaporation-control canister filter

Vacuum amplifier, EGR system

Spark-delay valve

Ported vacuum switch, EGR system

Temperature sensor, thermostatic air-cleaner

Choke vacuum-break

PCV filter

EGR valve

PCV valve

Electric element, automatic choke

A.I.R. pump

Deceleration-valve diaphragm

Figure 4–1   Emissions-control parts and systems

tem used in cars. Manufacturers began installing it early in the 1960s. Malfunctioning PCV components can cause excessive oil consumption, hard starting, stalling, rough idling, missing at slow speeds, and power loss. Parts that cause trouble are the PCV valve, hoses, and filter. Check them as follows:

1. Pull the PCV valve from the engine. In most cases, it's located in a rocker-arm cover. <u>Caution</u>: Be sure the engine is cold and not running.

2. Shake the valve. If it doesn't rattle, pull it off the hose, get a new valve of the same type, secure the new valve to the hose, and push it back into the engine.

3. If the valve you're testing passes the "shake" test, leave it connected to the hose, start the engine, and hold your thumb over the end of the valve. Your thumb should be drawn against the valve, indicating the presence of a vacuum. If you feel no suction (no vacuum), replace the valve and test again. If there is still no vacuum, remove the PCV hoses. In most cars, a hose runs between the air cleaner and rocker-arm cover, and another hose runs between the PCV valve and intake manifold or carburetor. Replace any cracked hose. If hoses are in good condition, clean out any carbon that may have accumulated inside them by pushing a dry cloth through each hose.

4. Find the PCV filter. In most cars it is inside the carburetor air cleaner, contained in a small metal housing on the side. Remove the filter from the housing and put in a new one. If there is no PCV filter in the carburetor air cleaner, look for it on the end of the PCV hose where the hose connects to the rocker-arm cover.

Chrysler uses an unusual PCV filter arrangement in many of its engines: a crankcase inlet air cleaner on the end of the PCV hose. To clean this filter, disconnect it from

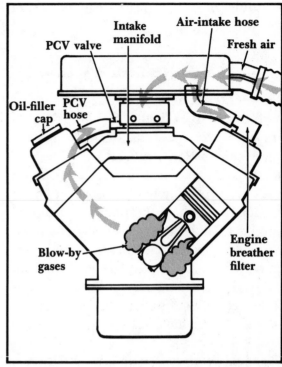

The positive-crankcase-ventilation system allows fresh air to mix with blow-by gases that result from burning fuel. This mixture enters the combustion chambers, where it is ignited and burned. If the system is working properly, no blow-by gases escape to pollute the atmosphere.

Figure 4–2   The positive-crankcase-ventilation system at work

the rocker-arm cover, detach the hose, and wash the filter in carburetor-and-choke cleaner. Then turn the filter upside down to let the solvent drain. Finally, fill the filter's housing with SAE 30 oil and reinstall the unit on the engine.

<u>Note</u>: Many imported and some domestically built engines, such as the Chrysler 2.2-liter and the Ford 1.6-liter, don't have traditional PCV systems. Instead of a PCV valve, they use a closed crankcase ventilation system with a fixed orifice through which crankcase gases enter the intake manifold. The part of this system that tends to clog and cause engine problems is the carburetor air-cleaner filter. Inspect and replace it, if necessary, as often as the maintenance

schedule in the owner's manual recommends.

Exhaust Gas Recirculation

The EGR system recirculates exhaust gas back through the intake manifold into the engine, where it acts as a cooling agent to lower combustion temperatures. This prevents oxides of nitrogen, which are pollutants, from forming in the engine and being expelled into the atmosphere. A malfunctioning EGR system can cause detonation, particularly when the engine is cold, hesitation or stalling on acceleration, and stalling on deceleration and during quick stops. It can also cause rough idling, hard starting, lack of power, and engine surge at a steady driving speed.

The heart of the system is the EGR valve, which is on the intake manifold near the carburetor (see Figure 4-3). You can check whether or not the system is working properly as follows. <u>Caution</u>: The EGR valve will be hot, so wear work gloves.

EGR Valve with an Exposed Diaphragm
With the engine warmed up and running at idle speed, the transmission in Park, and the parking brake engaged, place your gloved fingers under the EGR valve and feel for a rubber diaphragm. If you can't feel one, use the procedure given below for testing an EGR-valve diaphragm with a vacuum pump. But if your fingers come into contact with a diaphragm, have an assistant increase engine speed. The diaphragm should move up (open position) as the engine is accelerated, and down (closed position) as the engine returns to idle speed.

If the diaphragm doesn't move, pull the

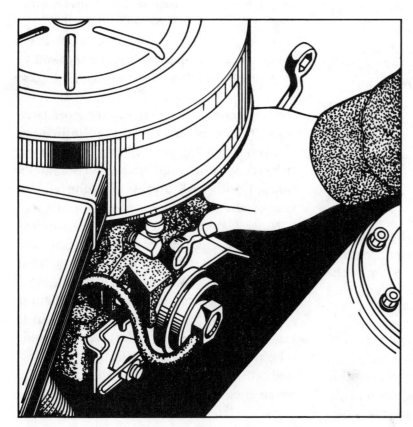

Figure 4–3   The exhaust-gas-recirculation valve

hose off the valve fitting and hold your finger over the hose opening. Accelerate to an engine speed of about 2,000 rpm for six- and eight-cylinder engines, or 3,000 rpm for four-cylinder engines.

If you feel a strong pull (vacuum), the EGR valve is faulty. Allow the engine to cool so that you don't burn yourself. Remove the bolts that hold the valve to the engine and replace the valve. (Many valves can be cleaned, but it's usually less bother and quite inexpensive to replace the valve.) If there is no vacuum, trace the hose to its other end to make sure it isn't kinked. Then pull it free from its fittings. Check the hose for cracks and be sure it isn't clogged. Replace a bad hose.

If the hose is free of kinks and in good condition, reconnect it securely and look to other EGR parts for the cause of the trouble. Other parts are all involved in recirculating exhaust gas at a temperature and time that won't adversely affect engine performance. These parts include a back-pressure variable transducer, temperature-control valve, vacuum amplifier, ported vacuum-switch, temperature vacuum-switch, temperature-sensor vacuum-valve, and engine-heat sensing valve. An engine will have some, but not all, of these. You'll need a repair manual to identify and test these components.

Testing an EGR Valve with a Vacuum Pump The diaphragms of valves on some General Motors engines are not exposed, so they can't be felt. These valves must be tested off the engine with a hand-held vacuum pump. Attach the hose of the vacuum pump to the EGR-valve vacuum-hose fitting and pump vacuum up. Most General Motors EGR valves are designed to retain vacuum until the vacuum source is disconnected. If the vacuum pump meter shows that the EGR valve assumes vacuum, but there is a drop in vacuum within 60 seconds, replace the EGR valve. If the EGR valve doesn't hold any vacuum at all, it may be bad or it may be a special valve used on a limited basis by General Motors. Consult a service manager at a GM dealership to determine what kind of valve your car has.

Thermostatic Air-Cleaner

Given different names by different manufacturers—Thermac Air Cleaner system by General Motors, Inlet Air Temperature system by Ford, and Heated Air Inlet system by Chrysler—this system keeps warm air flowing into the carburetor at all times, even when the ambient temperature is below zero. (Most imported-car manufacturers call the system the preheated intake-air system.)

Warm intake air curtails emissions by allowing a leaner (less fuel) carburetor setting and shorter choke time after cold starts. Problems caused when a part of this system fails include detonation, stalling, surging, power loss, hesitation, and a drop in fuel economy.

When a cold engine is started, a thermal-vacuum switch in the air cleaner lets vacuum (or suction) reach the air-door motor in the carburetor snorkel (see Figure 4-4). The motor pulls the door up, blocking off cold air from outside. (Depending on the engine, a duct may be connected from the snorkel to a source of outside air.) Air enters through the preheated-air opening and is heated by passing over and around the exhaust manifold. As the engine warms up, the thermal-vacuum switch gradually reduces vacuum to the air-door motor. The spring-loaded door starts to overcome the reduced vacuum and begins to close. When the engine is at operating temperature, the switch allows little or no vacuum to reach the air-door motor, so the door shuts completely.

Parts that can fail include the vacuum motor in the air-cleaner snorkel, the tem-

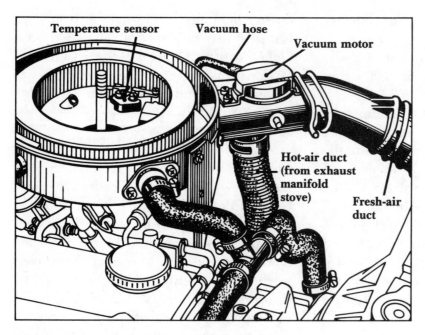

Temperature sensor   Vacuum hose   Vacuum motor

Hot-air duct
(from exhaust
manifold
stove)

Fresh-air
duct

Figure 4–4   A thermostatic air-cleaner system

perature sensor inside the air cleaner, and all ducts. If your engine doesn't have a conventional air cleaner and snorkel, consult the repair manual to find out where these parts are located.

The engine must be cold to check the system. If there's a duct over the end of the air-cleaner snorkel, unclamp and remove it. Start the engine and look inside the snorkel. (Use a mirror and flashlight if direct observation is difficult.) The valve in the snorkel should be up, sealing off the snorkel and thus blocking cold air from the fuel system. As the engine warms up, the valve in the snorkel should move down. If the valve functions, the system is operating properly. But if the valve doesn't move as the engine warms up, push it with a screwdriver. If the valve can be moved, shoot compressed air into the snorkel to blow out any dirt that may be causing the valve to bind. If compressed air doesn't free the valve, replace the valve by installing a new carburetor air-cleaner housing.

If the valve moves without binding when you push it with a screwdriver, but doesn't move of its own accord, pull the vacuum hose from the valve's vacuum motor. With the engine running at idle, hold your finger over the hose. If there is no suction (no vacuum), check the hose and each duct to make sure they are tightly connected and are kink- and crack-free. If your car has accordion ducts, look closely inside the folds; a hard-to-see tear may be allowing cold air into the system. A damaged duct or hose should be replaced.

If ducts and hose are in good shape, the cause of an inoperative thermostatic air-cleaner valve lies with a malfunctioning vacuum motor or temperature sensor. Check the motor by attaching a hand-held vacuum pump to the vacuum-motor's hose nipple. Apply 10 inches of mercury of vacuum and watch the vacuum-pump gauge. It should maintain the vacuum for 5 minutes. If it doesn't, replace the motor according to instructions in the repair manual. If it does, replace the temperature sensor according to instructions in the repair manual.

Fuel-Evaporation Control

This system has as its main element a charcoal-filled canister that you will find in the engine compartment. Hoses attached to it extend to the carburetor, fuel tank, and intake manifold. The system traps gasoline vapors that would otherwise escape into the atmosphere, and diverts them to the engine where they are burned.

A clogged or damaged fuel-evaporation control system causes an occasional odor of gasoline. A clogged or damaged system may also cause hard starting and rough idling when the engine is hot.

To resolve problems brought on by this system, check hoses for cracks. Replace damaged hoses with those specifically manufactured to handle fuel vapors (marked Evap or equivalent). Then, determine whether the charcoal canister has a replaceable filter in the bottom of the canister. Replace the filter. If there is no filter, you will have to replace the canister. (See chapter 1.) Generally, manufacturers suggest doing this every two years or 30,000 miles.

Other Emissions-Related Parts

The following discussion applies to engines that have carburetors. It is not applicable to engines equipped with electronic fuel injection.

Depending on the vehicle, a carburetor may be equipped with an idle-stop (antidieseling) solenoid, electrically-operated automatic choke, and a vacuum-break (or choke pull-off). Although these parts cannot technically be called emissions-control devices, without them emissions controls would tend to disrupt engine performance.

Idle-Stop Solenoid The idle-stop solenoid overcomes the tendency of some engines to run on (diesel) after the ignition is shut off. A high idle can abet that tendency to diesel, but many modern engines require a high idling speed for efficient operation of emissions controls. The idle-stop solenoid allows the throttle to close beyond the normal idle position when the ignition is turned off.

Note: Many engines have a device that resembles an idle-stop solenoid but that is activated by the air conditioner. It opens the throttle slightly when the air conditioner is on to prevent stalling, which the load imposed on the engine by the air conditioner's compressor can cause. Refer to the emissions control information label in the engine compartment to determine whether a solenoid on the carburetor is an antidieseling solenoid or an air conditioner speed-up solenoid.

The following procedure should be used to determine whether a defective idle-stop solenoid is causing dieseling, or whether a defective air conditioner speed-up solenoid is causing the engine to stall when the compressor is on:

1. Turn on the ignition switch, but don't start the engine. When testing an air conditioner speed-up solenoid, also turn on the air conditioner.

2. Watch the plunger at the throttle-lever end of the solenoid as you disconnect the electric wire connected to the solenoid. The plunger should draw away from the throttle lever. When you reconnect the electric wire, the plunger should extend and make contact with the lever.

3. If the plunger doesn't move, connect a 12-volt test light between the solenoid-wire terminal and a ground. If the light glows, showing that current is reaching the solenoid, the solenoid is defective. Replace it by unscrewing it from its bracket. If the light

doesn't glow, there is a problem with the wire or with the circuit feeding the wire. Use a volt/ohmmeter to test the wire for a short circuit.

Electric Choke and Vacuum-Break Most engines have an electrically operated automatic choke for more precise choke operation. They also have one or two vacuum-breaks to pull open choke valves slightly when a cold engine is started. When the electric element or vacuum-break malfunctions, stalling and poor fuel economy result.

Note: Dirt-encrusted choke linkages and choke valves cause many choke problems. Before testing the choke system, clean all choke linkages and valves by spraying them with carburetor-and-choke cleaner. Then check the choke and vacuum-break as follows:

1. With the engine cold and ambient temperature less than 80 degrees Fahrenheit, remove the carburetor air cleaner to observe the choke valve.

2. Have someone depress and then release the accelerator pedal. The choke valve should close over the carburetor throat.

3. Start the engine. The choke valve should open slightly. If not, turn off the engine, disconnect the hose attached to the choke vacuum-break, and connect a hand-held vacuum pump to the choke vacuum-break. Apply vacuum. If the choke vacuum-break doesn't assume or retain vacuum for 30 seconds, unbolt the part from the carburetor and replace it.

4. As the engine warms up, the choke valve should open fully. If not, check the electric choke element.

To test the electric choke element, disconnect the wire terminal at the element and connect a volt/ohmmeter between the terminal and a ground. Run the engine at idle. If the voltage is between 12 and 15 volts, replace the electric choke element as instructed in the repair manual. If the voltage is less than 12 volts, there is an open or shorted circuit. Check wire connections to make sure they are clean and tight. Then check wires for continuity with an ohmmeter. If you are not equipped to do this, leave it to a professional.

5

Hard Starting

TROUBLESHOOTING BRIEF

Having an engine that doesn't start, or that takes an exceptionally long period of cranking before it finally starts, is one of the most prevalent of all car problems. In order to approach troubleshooting logically, the conditions described in this chapter are placed into three categories:

1. Conditions that prevent an engine from making any noise as it's being cranked.

2. Conditions that allow an engine to make clicking sounds as it's being cranked or that cause an engine to crank too slowly to start.

3. Conditions that allow an engine to crank briskly, but which prevent it from starting.

In all but the last category, the malfunction causing the trouble lies with the car's ignition or cranking system. The cranking system consists of the battery, starter motor, starter solenoid, starter relay, neutral safety switch, and wiring. When the engine cranks normally but won't start, the trouble may be confined to the ignition system. If the problem isn't there, however, the fuel system or a mechanical defect inside the engine is to blame.

A particularly perplexing situation is an engine that starts promptly when it's cold, but not when it has warmed up. This type of starting problem is also discussed in a separate section.

Although not all information in this chapter applies to every make and model, much information applies no matter what kind of car you have—except for the section on hot-start problems. The information on hot-start problems does not cover cars with electronic fuel injection.

PROJECT DATA

Special tools and materials. Manufacturer's repair manual, 12-volt test lamp, battery-terminal puller, battery post- and terminal-cleaning tool, battery booster cables, hydrometer, vacuum pressure gauge, compression gauge, spark-plug gauge and gapping tool, insulated pliers, foam-backed household insulation, duct tape.

Possible replacement parts. Neutral safety switch, battery cable(s), battery, starter motor, starter solenoid, starter relay, wires associated with the starting system, spark plugs, rotor, distributor cap, carburetor insulation block, thermostatically controlled electric fan, EGR valve.

Tasks that require two people. Testing for current to the neutral safety switch; checking the fuel system; testing for ignition system current; starting a flooded engine.

Job difficulty and time. Degree of difficulty is relative to the mechanic's experience; all times are approximate.

• Testing the battery: Easy, a few seconds to 10 minutes depending on whether the battery is maintenance-free or not.
• Cleaning and tightening or replacing battery terminals and cables: Easy, 15–30 minutes.
• Testing the starter motor and starter solenoid: Difficult, 60–90 minutes.
• Replacing the starter relay: Moderately difficult, 30 minutes.
• Testing the neutral safety switch: Moderately difficult, 15 minutes.
• Replacing the neutral safety switch: Moderately difficult, 30 minutes.
• Replacing the neutral safety switch to starter solenoid wire: Difficult, 60–90 minutes.

• Testing the fuel supply to the carburetor: Easy, 10 minutes.
• Spark intensity test: Easy, 10–15 minutes.
• Replacing spark plugs: Easy to moderately difficult, depending on engine, 30–45 minutes.
• Testing the choke system: Easy, 10–20 minutes.
• Cleaning the choke system: Easy, 10 minutes.
• Testing engine compression: Easy to moderately difficult, depending on the engine, 30–60 minutes.
• Testing the EGR valve: Easy to moderately difficult, depending on the type of EGR valve, 10–30 minutes.
• Replacing the EGR valve: Easy, 15–30 minutes.
• Tracking down the reason for an intermittent hot-starting condition: Easy to moderately difficult, 90–120 minutes.
• Checking for unsecured vacuum hoses: Easy, 20–30 minutes.
• Insulating fuel system components from heat: Easy if components don't have to be removed, moderately difficult if you have to remove the carburetor: 30–60 minutes.

Safety precautions. Fuel in, and fuel vapors from, the fuel-delivery system and carburetor and the hydrogen gas given off by a battery ignite easily and are highly explosive. When working on a car, never smoke or bring an open flame or device that creates sparks near the car. Work outdoors, not in an enclosed space, and always keep a dry chemical (class B) fire extinguisher nearby.

• When cranking the engine, make sure the parking brake is fully engaged or your foot is firmly on the brake pedal and the transmission is in Park (automatic) or Neutral (manual).

• When working on or around the battery, wear safety goggles and rubber gloves. If battery acid should get on your skin, flush the area with cool water for at least 5 minutes. Consult a physician at once if battery acid gets in your eye.

• When working in the engine compartment, make sure the ignition is off unless instructions state otherwise. If a test requires that the engine be cranked or run, keep your hands away from moving parts such as the fan and pulleys.

• Do not wear loose clothing when working under the hood. Also, remove rings and your watch.

• To prevent electrical sparks, disconnect the negative battery terminal when performing any test that does not require you to crank the engine.

• When doing a spark-intensity test, keep the sparking end of the spark-plug cable away from the carburetor, which exudes fuel vapors. To avoid shocks, hold the cable using an insulated spark-plug cable pliers, never in your hand.

• With a spark-plug or distributor-to-ignition-coil cable disconnected, crank the engine for no more than two seconds. Prolonged cranking may damage the catalytic converter.

When Your Engine Won't Start

Starting is the most basic automotive malfunction and correcting the problem can save you the cost and inconvenience of paying for a towing service, a mechanic's service call, or both. Starting systems operate on the same principle, with many possible variations.

For example, in a typical General Motors circuit (see Figure 5-1), battery current is always available at the battery-cable connection at the starter solenoid. Lights and other electrical devices can receive power from this terminal, whether or not the ignition is

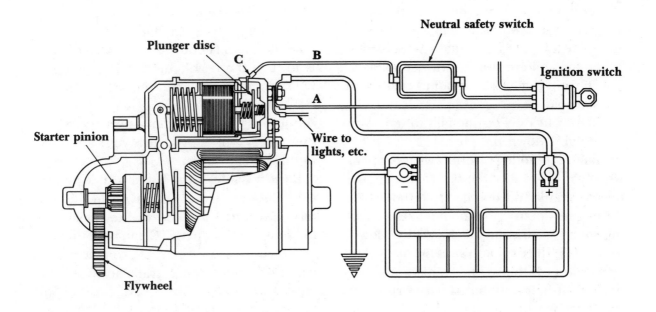

Figure 5-1 Typical General Motors starting system

43

switched on. When the ignition switch is turned to the Start position, current flows from small wire A at the solenoid-battery terminal through the ignition switch and along wire B to the solenoid terminal C. From there, current flows through an electrical magnet that pulls the solenoid against the solenoid-switch contacts. When the solenoid-plunger disc touches the contacts, battery current flows to the starter-motor, causing the motor to turn. At the same time, the shift lever, which is attached to the solenoid plunger, causes the starter pinion to move in and engage the flywheel. When the flywheel engages, the engine cranks.

Other car manufacturers use slightly different systems. Ford mounts its starter solenoid on the fender wall. The solenoid sends battery current to a positive-engagement starter motor that has a movable shoe attached to the starter's pinion gear. When the key is turned to Start, current flows through the starter's electromagnet. The shoe is drawn to the magnet, thus engaging the starter pinion with the flywheel.

Chrysler cars use a solenoid to engage the starter pinion gear with the flywheel. Unlike the General Motors system, however, a starter relay is used to actuate the solenoid. When the ignition switch is turned to Start, the starter relay closes, sending current to the solenoid.

When your car's engine fails to start, you can narrow down the possible reasons for the failure by noting carefully what happens when you try to start the car: (1) the engine doesn't crank and doesn't make noise; (2) the engine doesn't crank, but makes a clicking sound, or the engine cranks too slowly to start; (3) the engine cranks normally, but won't start; (4) the engine cranks and starts normally when cold, but is hard or impossible to start when it's hot.

Engine Doesn't Crank and Doesn't Make Noise

If you turn the key to the start position and nothing happens—the engine doesn't crank and there is no noise—first try a simple adjustment. With an automatic transmission, make certain the gear-shift selector is in Park. With a manual shift, make sure you have pressed the clutch pedal all the way to the floor. If you don't do whichever is applicable to your car, the neutral safety switch (also referred to as the neutral start switch) will keep the engine from cranking.

If the transmission is in Park, move the shift lever through the gears and put it in Park again. If the transmission is a manual shift and you have pressed the clutch pedal against the floor, release the clutch and press it down a couple of times. The neutral safety switch is a mechanical switch and may occasionally fail to make contact. Manipulating the shift lever or clutch pedal may restore contact. If it doesn't, the switch should be tested and replaced if found to be defective (see page 46).

The next step in troubleshooting an engine that doesn't crank and makes no noise is to turn the headlights on. If they don't light, the most likely reasons are a bad battery or a loose or corroded battery-cable connector. Test the battery (see page 26). If the battery works well, turn your attention to the battery cables.

Battery Cables Use battery-cable pullers to remove the battery cables from the battery; disconnect the negative terminal first to avoid creating sparks. Clean both the battery terminals and the cable connectors. A battery-cleaning tool, available from an automotive parts store, works best if your battery has posts. The tool contains a tapered wire brush that's used to clean cable connectors and another brush inside a case that fits over the posts. You clean the posts by twisting the tool. If your battery has side terminals, use a piece of sandpaper to clean cable connectors. Reconnect the cables (positive cable first), making sure each is clean and tight at both ends.

If headlights go on, but dim when the ignition switch is turned to start the engine, the most likely causes are a bad battery or starting system part. Check the battery (see chapter 3); then, the starter-system circuit.

Starter-System Circuit If the headlights go on and do not dim when you turn the ignition switch to the Start position, there is a defect in the starter circuit. Likely suspects are a loose or broken wire, a bad starter solenoid, or a bad neutral safety switch.

Check first to see if any wire is loose, broken, or disconnected at the starter relay (if your car has one) and at the starter solenoid. As discussed, some cars have both a starter relay and starter solenoid; others have only a starter solenoid.

With all wires secure, find out next if current is reaching the starter solenoid. On Ford cars the solenoid is most often found on the fender well, usually close to the battery. On most other cars, the solenoid is attached to the starter.

Locate the large cable that connects the battery to the solenoid; it is the positive cable from the battery. A much smaller wire connects to the solenoid near the positive cable. This wire runs to the ignition switch and actuates the starter solenoid when the switch is in the start position. Hold the probe of a 12-volt test lamp against the small-wire connection at the solenoid and ground the test lamp lead (see Figure 5-2). Have an assistant turn the ignition switch to crank the engine. The lamp should light.

If it lights with a General Motors or Chrysler car, the problem lies in the solenoid or starter motor. At this point the solenoid and starter motor must be removed

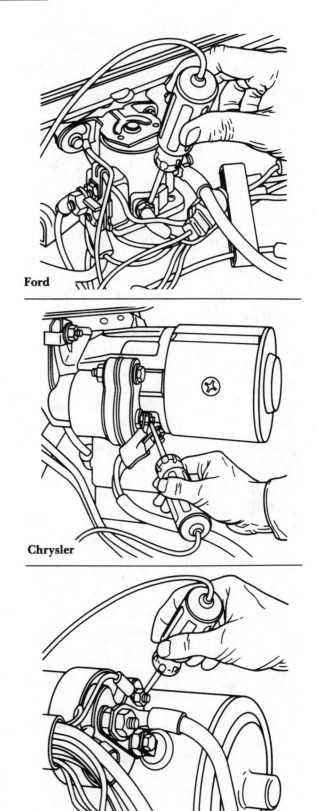

Ford

Chrysler

GM

Figure 5–2 Testing the solenoid switch

and tested on a workbench using a voltammeter that can impose an electrical load. With Ford cars, if the test lamp lights and there is no noise, replace the solenoid.

Note: If you don't have the manufacturer's repair manual, let a professional mechanic test the starter solenoid and starter motor. The testing procedure and specifications differ from car to car.

Neutral Safety Switch If the test lamp doesn't light, test the neutral safety switch by bypassing it with a jumper wire (see Figure 5-3). But before you set up the bypass, engage the parking brake and place an automatic transmission in Park or a manual transmission in Neutral.

To bypass the neutral safety switch in a Chrysler car, remove the G wire from the starter relay and use a jumper wire to connect the G-wire terminal to a ground. Turn the ignition switch to Start. If the engine cranks, either the transmission linkage needs adjustment in order for it to actuate the safety switch properly, or the neutral safety switch needs replacement. With General Motors cars, remove the two-wire disconnect from the safety switch (safety switch wires are usually purple) and bridge the gap with a paper clip.

With other makes of car, either domestic or imported, the principle is the same. Locate the wires running to and from the neutral safety switch, disconnect them, and then connect them together with a jumper wire or paper clip. If you use a paper clip, check that you have made a good connection. Do not hold the paper clip when the car is cranked. If the switch connections are underneath the car, do not remain there while the engine is cranked. Should the car roll, it could run over you.

If the engine cranks when you bypass the neutral safety switch, the switch is bad. Replace it.

Repair Tip: The neutral safety switch is

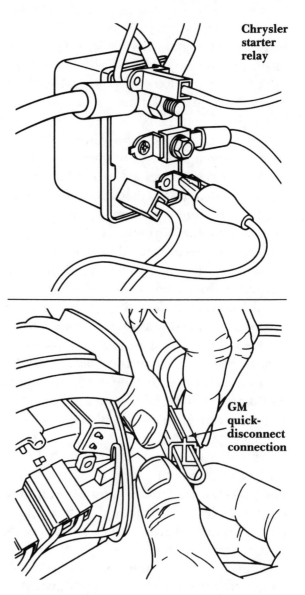

Chrysler starter relay

GM quick-disconnect connection

Figure 5–3 Bypassing the neutral safety switch

located on the steering column or on the transmission. Use your repair manual to find it. To install a new switch, disconnect the negative cable from the battery and detach wires from the neutral safety switch. Unscrew the switch, install a new switch, and reconnect wires and the battery negative cable.

Ignition-Switch Circuit If the engine still doesn't crank after bypassing the neutral safety switch, use a 12-volt test lamp to determine whether current is reaching the neutral safety switch.

To do this with Ford and General Motors cars, remove the two-wire quick-disconnect connector, which may be located at the switch or somewhere along the two wires leading to the switch. With the test lamp grounded to the vehicle and a friend holding the ignition switch in the start position, touch the test-lamp probe inside both wire terminals of the quick-disconnect. The lamp should light when it's touched to one of the terminals. If the lamp doesn't light, the problem is either a bad ignition switch or a bad wire to the switch. If the test lamp lights at one of the quick-disconnect terminals and the engine still won't crank, the problem is in the wire running from the neutral safety switch to the small-wire terminal of the solenoid.

Note: If you can get at both ends of the wire running from the neutral safety switch to the starter motor, you should be able to disconnect the wire and install a new wire (make sure to match the wire gauge exactly). But since replacing the ignition switch involves disassembly of the steering column, a mechanic who has the special equipment necessary for removing the steering wheel should do this job.

Cars made by Chrysler use a starter relay in addition to a starter solenoid. If the engine doesn't crank after bypassing the starter relay with jumper wires, find out if current is reaching the relay.

With the G terminal of the relay grounded with a jumper wire, touch the probe of a test lamp to the I terminal of the relay. (Chrysler relay terminals are marked with letters.) Connect the test-lamp wire to a ground. If the test lamp lights when the ignition switch is turned to crank the engine, but the starter doesn't crank, the relay is bad. Replace it.

Repair Tip: To replace a starter relay in a Chrysler car, disconnect the negative cable from the battery and wires from the relay. Then unbolt the relay.

If the test lamp doesn't light, there's a problem with the ignition switch or the wire running from the relay to the ignition switch. Usually, the neutral safety switch is the cause of the problem. Test the switch by bypassing it as previously explained.

Engine Makes Clicking Sounds or Cranks Too Slowly

If the engine makes a clicking noise or a series of clicks when you turn the key to start the car, the cause is usually a weak battery or a bad cable connection. Remove the battery cables (negative cable first) at the battery and clean them (see page 44). Then reconnect the cables (positive cable first) to the battery and check them at their other ends. A cable that is loose or corroded at the starter or ground end can create the same problem as one that's loose or corroded at the battery.

After servicing the cables, boost the battery to get the engine started (see Figure 5-4). Attach a jumper cable to the positive post of the bad battery, then attach the other end of the cable to the positive post of the good battery. Attach one end of the other jumper to a good ground in the engine compartment of the disabled car and the other end to a good ground in the engine compartment of the car with the good battery. Start the engine of the car with the good battery, then try to start the other car. When you disconnect the jumper cables, reverse the sequence. Watch out for moving pulleys, belts, and fan blades as you disconnect the cables. If after jump starting the car the clicking continues when you try to start it, the battery is weak. Follow the procedures given in chapter 3.

A Single Click If when you turn the ig-

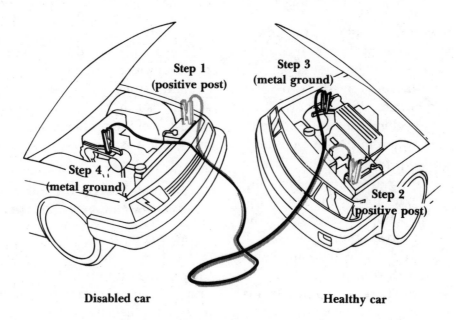

Figure 5–4   Jump-starting a car

nition key to crank the engine you get a single click rather than a series of them, clean the battery cable terminals. If cables are clean and tight and the battery is fully charged, the problem is either a bad starter motor or starter solenoid. To determine which, use jumper cables to bypass the solenoid. If the bypass allows the starter motor to work, the solenoid is bad. If the starter motor doesn't work, then the starter is bad.

Slow Cranking   If the engine turns over slowly, but won't start, the problem usually is a bad battery or starter. First, check battery cable connections and the battery. If cable and connections are good and the engine still turns over slowly, a bad starter is probably the culprit. But check the mounting bolts that hold the starter in position. Occasionally, bolts will loosen and allow the starter to tilt at an angle. In that position, the starter cannot turn the engine over fast enough to start it. If bolts are loose, tighten them, and try again. If the engine still cranks slowly with the starter mounted securely, you should replace the starter.

Engine Cranks But Won't Start

Check the fuel supply first when an engine cranks at normal speed but doesn't start. If there's gas in the tank, find out next whether fuel is reaching the engine. Remove the air cleaner and move the accelerator linkage or have an assistant pump the gas pedal several times. You should see gas squirting into the carburetor. If no gas squirts out, troubleshoot the fuel system (see chapter 1). If fuel does squirt into the carburetor, however, lack of fuel isn't the cause of the no-start condition. Check for spark.

Spark-Intensity Test   Remove a spark plug wire from a spark plug by rotating the boot back and forth until it loosens. Then pull up on the boot to remove it from the spark plug. Caution: Pull only on the boot— not on the wire, which will break. (Use spark-plug cable pliers if you have a pair.)

Insert a screwdriver that has an insulated handle into the boot so the screwdriver touches the metal terminal inside the boot. Hold the shank of the screwdriver about ¼ inch from a clean metal part (a ground) and have someone crank the engine.

If a bright blue spark doesn't jump the space between the screwdriver and ground, see "Lack of Spark" (below). If, however, there is spark, remove the spark plugs to see if they are wet with gasoline. If they are wet, fuel is not igniting; likely causes are an improper starting procedure, faulty spark plugs, or a defective carburetor part.

The Starting Procedure Follow the starting procedure recommended in your owner's manual. The usual recommendations follow: Press the accelerator pedal to the floor once, remove your foot from the pedal, and crank the engine for no more than 15 seconds. If the engine doesn't start, let it rest for 15 seconds and try again. Now if the engine doesn't start, look elsewhere for the cause of the wet spark plug.

Spark Plug Gap Remove each spark plug and examine the electrodes for signs of pitting or corrosion. Check the gap and see if you can adjust it to specification. If the electrodes are worn or if you cannot adjust the gap, install a new set after gapping them to specification.

Refer to the vehicle emissions control information decal on the radiator shroud or to the repair manual to find out the manufacturer's specified spark-plug gap. Adjust each plug to specification by bending the side electrode with the bending adapter of a spark-plug adjusting tool. <u>Caution:</u> Use no other tool. You will damage the plugs.

To check the gap, insert a wire feeler gauge of the recommended size between the two electrodes and move it back and forth. The plug is properly gapped when the feeler gauge moves, offering slight resistance.

The Carburetor If spark plugs are in good condition and gapped properly, you may be faced with a carburetor problem. A sticking choke plate is a common one. Be-

fore checking the choke plate, be sure the engine is cold. Then remove the top of the air cleaner and have an assistant in the car pump the accelerator pedal once. The choke plate should close over the carburetor throat. If it doesn't, the choke mechanism should be repaired as outlined in the repair manual.

If the choke plate closes, open the choke plate by moving the accelerator linkage and pressing the lower edge of the plate. The choke plate should open to vertical position. There will be some resistance from the choke's bimetal spring as you do this, but the plate should open smoothly with no binding. Release the choke plate. It should snap shut quickly and smoothly.

If the choke plate sticks, the cause (a bent or dirty linkage) must be eliminated and the choke adjusted to specification. Your repair manual explains how to adjust the choke, but unless you're an experienced mechanic, let a professional work on the carburetor.

If the choke is working properly, reinstall the air cleaner. Push the accelerator pedal to the floor to trip the choke unloader, which will allow the choke to open. Hold the pedal against the floor. Don't pump it. Crank the engine for 15 seconds. If the engine doesn't start, wait 15 seconds while still holding the accelerator pedal to the floor; then try again for 15 seconds. If after three or four tries the engine doesn't start, look at the carburetor. All the fuel can leak out of a cracked carburetor float bowl, or out of one that has a porous casting, when the vehicle is parked for a few hours. The engine must be cranked excessively, until the float bowl fills again, before the car will start. If there is gas around the carburetor's base, it is damaged and should be replaced. Consult the repair manual for details but again, let a professional mechanic handle the repair if you lack the necessary experience.

Lack of Spark If you check for spark

and there is none, or the spark is yellow rather than blue, remove the high-tension cable from the center tower of the distributor cap. Use insulated spark-plug pliers to hold the end of the cable ¼ inch from a clean metal part of the engine (ground) and have an assistant crank the engine.

If a blue spark now jumps the gap, the distributor rotor or cap is damaged. A visual inspection will indicate which must be replaced; look for cracks and burn marks in both parts. If no spark jumps the gap or the spark is yellow instead of blue, there is a problem in the ignition circuit, such as a bad resistor, pickup coil, or module (see chapter 2).

If the ignition and fuel systems pass your tests, then the reason for the failure to start lies inside the engine. Make a compression test and compare the readings you get with the specifications given in the repair manual.

Compression When testing engine compression, disconnect and ground the high tension cable at the ignition coil and remove all spark plugs. Push or screw the compression gauge firmly into each spark plug port to assure that no compression is lost as the engine is cranked. When you've taken all readings from every cylinder, compare them to the compression specification given in the repair manual and follow the guidelines given in that manual concerning what is and what isn't adequate compression. For example, low compression on all cylinders indicates a bad timing chain, timing gears, or piston rings. In any case, engine repair is called for.

Hot-Start Problems

Typically, a hot-start problem reveals itself as follows: The engine starts promptly first thing in the morning or after the car has been sitting idle for a few hours. But after being driven for a while, shut off, and parked for an hour or less, the engine refuses to restart. What causes the problem?

In most cases, heat is affecting either the fuel delivery or the ignition system. Your immediate concern is to get the car started and go home. But even if one of the immediate fixes given below works for you all the time, it is a nuisance having an engine that balks at starting whenever that engine is warm. There are also ways for you to fix the problem permanently.

Note: The repairs described here do not apply to engines with fuel injection. When a warm engine equipped with a fuel-injection system balks at starting, try a different brand of gasoline. If that change doesn't solve the problem, ask a mechanic to do a fuel-system-pressure test when the engine is warmed up. The test can determine whether a malfunctioning fuel-pressure regulator or a leaking fuel injector is causing the problem.

Immediate Fixes First, assume the engine is flooded with gas. Press the accelerator pedal down to the floor and hold it there to keep the throttle and choke plates open wide and allow air to enter the engine. If the engine is flooded, air will dilute the gas and should get you started. When the engine catches, quickly back off on the gas pedal to prevent the engine from racing.

If the engine fails to catch, do not keep cranking the engine. You will run down the battery. Next, take a passive approach. Open the hood and let the vehicle sit for half an hour to cool off. Chances are that heat has caused the engine to flood. An open hood will allow heat to dissipate, and you should be able to get going.

If you still can't get started, more drastic action is necessary. Remove the air cleaner to make sure the choke plate is open (see page 49). If not, an inoperative choke is causing your problem, and you need to keep the choke plate open so you can get started. Open the plate by hand and wedge the handle of a screwdriver between the plate and carburetor throat. This will do temporarily, but to repair the problem permanently the choke thermostatic spring will have to be replaced as described in the repair manual.

Raw Fuel If the choke works well and can be ruled out as the cause of the trouble, look for raw fuel in the carburetor and intake manifold. Hold the choke and throttle plates open with a long stick or screwdriver. Then look down into the carburetor (a flashlight is helpful).

If you see drops of gasoline, you are faced with one of two problems. First, engine heat could have caused the fuel to boil inside the carburetor. This creates excessive pressure that forces the float needle off its seat. An unseated needle, in turn, allows too much gas to be pushed out the carburetor jets, causing the engine to flood (see Figure 5-5). Under normal circumstances, the amount of gas metered into the carburetor is precisely controlled by the needle valve. Metering insures that the carburetor won't be under- or oversupplied, despite changes in demand made on it by the engine.

A leak inside the carburetor can also cause raw gas to puddle in the carburetor and intake manifold. A carburetor leak poses a more serious problem: the carburetor must be replaced.

Hot-start Lean Conditions The opposite of a hot-start flooding problem is a hot-start lean condition. Actually, an engine will seldom have a lean condition that prevents it from starting. If the fuel mixture is lean, the engine should start, but is then likely to stall.

There are three probable causes for a lean condition: (1) the vehicle may be out of gas;

(2) heat may have vaporized the fuel in either the fuel line or fuel pump, and the pump won't pull the vapor; (3) one or more vacuum hoses may have fallen off.

There are easy ways to check the first two. Check the fuel gauge, then take the air cleaner off the carburetor and peek into the carburetor throat. Move the throttle by hand. You should see fuel squirt into the throat. No squirt indicates vapor lock (see below). Nevertheless, fuel gauges can be inaccurate. If, after letting the engine cool further, the car still doesn't start, you may simply be out of gas.

If one or more of the vacuum hoses has come off, the decrease in the vacuum in the manifold reduces the engine's ability to draw enough fuel from the carburetor. Check to see that all vacuum lines are connected and in good condition.

Vacuum hoses are connected at one end to vacuum ports on the carburetor or intake manifold. With the engine cold, trace each hose from its circuit port to its terminus at the other end, which may be at a variety of valves or motors. Check to see that the hose isn't cracked and is securely fastened at each end.

If you can't find a fuel problem, the trouble lies in the electrical system. You can make one check immediately.

Electrical System If the starter motor seems to be turning over too slowly to start the engine, have an assistant hold the ignition key in the start position. *Carefully* touch all four end connections of the battery cables, feeling for heat. Caution: Stay away from moving parts, and bring your finger to each point slowly and carefully, withdrawing it if you feel excessive heat. If a cable connection is too hot to touch, you've located the troublemaker. Cables may look fine on the outside, but can be corroded under the sheathing. Replace the cable (see page 28).

Fixing Fuel Problems

If you found raw fuel in the carburetor or intake manifold, or you were able to start the engine by holding the gas pedal on the floor, it indicates vapor lock or an overly rich fuel condition. The carburetor or fuel line is getting too hot and fuel is vaporizing, or the carburetor is out of adjustment.

Observe where the exhaust manifold and exhaust pipes are located relative to heat-sensitive parts such as the carburetor, fuel pump, and fuel line. For instance, does the pipe out of the exhaust manifold run close to a fuel line? If so, you'll have to do something about blocking or dispersing the heat.

There are simple ways to keep fuel-delivery components cool. To protect the fuel line, wrap the line with foam-backed household insulation that you can buy in a hardware store. Wind duct tape around the insulation to secure it. You can also wrap the fuel pump to keep it from overheating.

If the carburetor overheats, a special gasket, called an insulation block, can be installed under it. The block raises the carburetor about ¼ inch off the hot engine. The fiberglass pad on the underside of the hood may be trapping heat; removing it can help lower engine-compartment temperature. You could also have an electric fan installed in the engine compartment. The fan is thermostatically controlled to switch itself on at a predesignated temperature.

If your hot-start problem isn't caused by overheating and fuel vaporization, the carburetor may be out of adjustment. But getting it adjusted correctly can pose problems. Many mechanics still believe they can make accurate adjustments by listening and turning a screw or two. That won't work. Some of the more sophisticated carburetors have over a dozen levers and rods as well as five or six spring-loaded or thermostatically-controlled fulcrums. A proper carburetor adjustment takes 30 to 45 minutes using the right equipment and the factory service manual. The adjustments must be checked cold, hot, and in the heat-soak position (after the hot engine is turned off).

Suppose you've determined that your problem is neither fuel vaporization nor flooding; instead, you suspect a hot-start lean condition. The exhaust-gas-recirculation (EGR) valve may be stuck open, reducing vacuum to the carburetor jets and causing a lean condition (see Figure 5-5). Check for a stuck valve with a vacuum gauge.

Attach the vacuum gauge to any convenient vacuum port on the carburetor or intake manifold by first disconnecting the vacuum hose from the port. Crank the engine with the throttle plate closed. The gauge should read about 17 to 21 inches of mercury. If not, *gently* tap the side of the EGR valve with a hammer while the engine is running. If you notice that the idle smooths out, the EGR valve has reached the limits of its useful life. Replace it.

Let the engine get cold. Then disconnect the vacuum hose from the EGR valve. Remove the bolts (there are usually two) that are holding the valve to the engine and install the new EGR valve.

Fixing Electrical Problems

Install a new cable if you found a hot end connection on one of the battery cables when you investigated them. If cables were relatively cool, however, and the starter sounds weak and sluggish, check the starter solenoid next.

The starter solenoid is supposed to pull a copper disc across two copper lugs to make a connection and deliver current to the starter motor. On some models, particularly in General Motors vehicles, engineers had

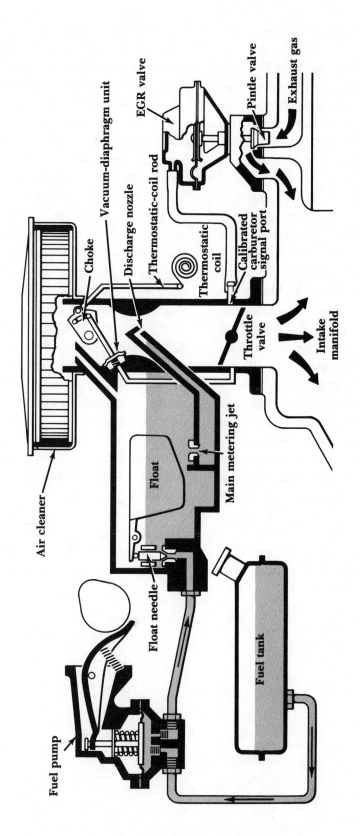

Figure 5–5   The exhaust-gas-recirculation and fuel-delivery systems

trouble getting the starter pinion to back out of the ring gear. They used a heavier retractor spring that solved the pinion problem. But the solenoid has to compress that spring to make the electrical contact. A strong spring prevents good contact, and the starter will turn slowly because it does not get enough current. The cure for this problem: a weaker solenoid spring. Auto electrical shops carry them. <u>Note:</u> Most auto electrical shops are aware of the cars equipped with starter solenoids with springs that are too strong.

If the problem isn't in the solenoid, it may be in the design of the starter system itself. Normal engine temperature for most engines is 250 degrees Fahrenheit or more. When you park the car after a drive, engine temperature goes up another 15 or 20 degrees. At those high temperatures, closely fitted aluminum pistons get squeezed in the bores, and the starter motor strains to turn over. The starter's electrical draw rises dramatically, robbing current from the ignition system. A starter that has weakened cannot cope with these conditions. Therefore, have a starter-draw test performed to check starter power.

Because the test calls for a special tool called a carbon-pile rheostat as well as a voltammeter, this procedure is best left to a service garage. High draw means the starter is weak and should be replaced.

Ignition Wiring One final condition may be the most difficult to uncover. If the engine cranks well when it's hot, and you find neither evidence of a too-rich or too-lean condition, nor cable- or starter-circuit trouble, the cause of the hot-start problem may be in your ignition wiring. If you heat a wire, its resistance to electrical flow increases. Resistors, capacitors, and coils become old, oxidized, and more resistant as well. Even though they work well enough when cold, they do not function effectively when hot. Resistance increase may be one of the toughest problems to defeat, since it only occurs when components are hot.

To catch it, start the engine when it's cold. Then, blow heat from a hair dryer on one ignition component at a time—the ignition coil, distributor, control module, and so forth. Apply heat for at least 5 minutes. If the engine stalls and won't restart, the component you're heating becomes suspect. Have it replaced.

<u>Important:</u> If you don't uncover a heat-sensitive component within 15 minutes, turn the engine off and let it cool for at least one hour before further testing.

6

Detonation and Preignition

TROUBLESHOOTING BRIEF

Rattling and pinging sounds emanating from your car's engine can sometimes be normal. At other times, however, they may signal serious and destructive conditions. You can learn how to recognize normal and abnormal detonation (also called spark knock, ping, and autoignition). You can also learn how to distinguish between detonation and preignition. Preignition sounds similar to detonation, but it is never normal.

Detonation often accompanies stressful acceleration of the engine. It should not alarm you as long as it falls into the definition of "harmless detonation" as given in the chapter. In fact, trying to get rid of an occasional spark knock may prove fruitless and could end up costing you time and money.

Abnormal detonation and preignition have different causes. But the result is the same: serious engine damage in the form of ruined piston assemblies and cylinder heads.

This chapter is organized to allow you to find the reason for an abnormal detonation or preignition in your engine, so you can take steps to avoid major damage. After an explanation of the differences between normal detonation, abnormal detonation, and preignition, you'll find a chart that provides a step-by-step procedure to help you track down the cause of the problem.

Note: This chapter is devoted to troubleshooting. It is not intended to help you repair a problem once the reason for it has been identified. Many of the repair tasks, such as replacing spark plugs, are simple. For others, you will need the specific instructions provided by the manufacturer's repair manual for your vehicle. Still others, such as replacing a head gasket, are very involved. Unless you are an experienced mechanic, leave those to a professional mechanic.

This chapter does not cover electronic fuel injection. Other systems of a car with EFI can be checked using the guidelines in this chapter.

PROJECT DATA

Special tools and materials. Manufacturer's repair manual, engine carbon-deposit solvent, heat-control-valve solvent, cooling-system pressure tester, hand-held vacuum pump, vacuum/pressure gauge, timing light, tachometer, ohmmeter.

Possible replacement parts. Spark plugs; radiator cap; drive belt; duct, hose, motor, thermal-vacuum switch, and door of the air-door system of the carburetor air-cleaner; exhaust manifold; vacuum valve and thermal-vacuum switch of the heat-control valve; carburetor gasket; head gasket; EGR valve; any one of the various sensors used as part of the engine electronic control system.

Job difficulty and time. Degree of difficulty is relative to the mechanic's experience; all times are approximate.

- Inspecting spark plugs: Easy to moderately difficult, depending on the engine, 30–45 minutes.
- Draining excess oil: Easy, 15–20 minutes.
- Inspecting routing of spark plug cables: Easy, 10 minutes.
- Inspecting the thermostatic air-cleaner: Easy, 20 minutes.
- Lubricating heat-control valve: Easy, 10 minutes.
- Checking ignition timing, vacuum-advance, and centrifugal advance: Moderately difficult, 30–45 minutes.
- Inspecting the EGR valve: Easy to moderately difficult, depending on the type of EGR valve, 10–30 minutes.
- Testing for an air leak: Easy, 15 minutes.
- Testing for a blown head gasket: Easy, 10 minutes.

- Inspecting exhaust system: Easy, 10 minutes.
- Checking the cooling system: Moderately difficult, 90 minutes.
- Testing sensors: Moderately difficult, 45 minutes.

Safety precautions. Fuel and fuel vapors are highly flammable and explosive; batteries give off hydrogen gas that can explode when ignited by a spark or flame. Therefore, when working on a car, never smoke or bring a device that can create sparks near the car.

- Work outdoors, not in an enclosed space, and always keep a dry chemical (class B) fire extinguisher nearby.
- To prevent electrical sparks, disconnect the negative battery terminal when performing any test that does not require you to crank the engine.
- Watch out for pulleys and belts when the engine is running; never wear loose clothing, watches, rings, or other jewelry when working on a car.

Detonation and Preignition

Detonation results when two energy forces collide in a combustion chamber. The severity of this collision determines whether detonation threatens to do serious damage to the engine or whether it is harmless. Under certain conditions, engines are designed to operate with a faint ticking sound known as trace detonation. But abnormal detonation over a fairly long period of time can destroy the pistons, the connecting rods, and the cylinder head and lead to huge repair bills.

Preignition is a separate but related problem. It is never normal and can very quickly cause major engine damage. There's no such thing as "trace preignition."

During normal combustion, the spark plug ignites the fuel mixture (see A in Figure 6-1). The resulting flame front races evenly across the combustion chamber (B and C) until all fuel is burned (D). At the start of detonation (see Figure 6-2), the spark plug ignites the fuel mixture (A), which begins to burn normally (B). Increasing pressure and temperature then cause an unburned portion of the mixture to ignite

(C). The flame fronts from the two burning pockets of fuel meet violently (D), releasing energy that causes the cylinder head to vibrate with a knocking or pinging sound. Power loss may result. At the start of preignition (see Figure 6-3), a red-hot carbon deposit in the combustion chamber (A)—rather than a spark plug—ignites the fuel mixture. The flame front spreads (B), causing a temperature increase sufficient to ig-

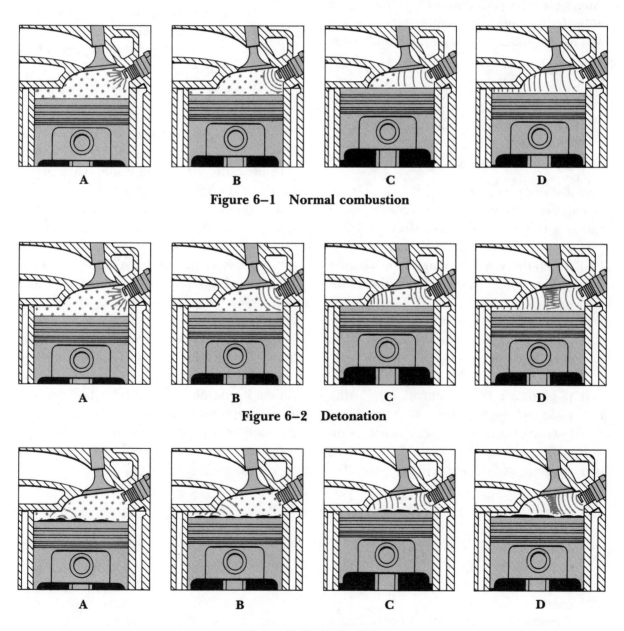

A	B	C	D

Figure 6–1   Normal combustion

A	B	C	D

Figure 6–2   Detonation

A	B	C	D

Figure 6—3   Preignition

nite pockets of the mixture in other parts of the cylinder (C). Preignition can occur when the piston has not reached the top of its stroke, which subjects the piston and connecting rod to destructive mechanical and thermal forces from colliding flame fronts (D).

Harmless Detonation

Pinging or a ticking sound from the engine indicate harmless trace detonation when you hear it under the following conditions:

- when the throttle is opened or closed rapidly;
- when the engine is cold;
- when the vehicle is climbing a steep hill or in any other situation that requires wide-open throttle;
- when the brake pedal is pressed.

The last situation occurs because some cars have an exhaust-gas-recirculation (EGR) system cutout switch that shuts off EGR when the brakes are applied. Because the EGR system normally feeds the cylinders exhaust gas in order to lower temperature, the temperature increase that results when EGR is cut off causes temporary, but harmless, trace detonation.

Although it's not harmful, you may be able to eliminate trace detonation by using fuel having a higher octane rating than what you're now using. The octane rating is an index of gasoline's antiknock properties; high octane does not increase power or make an engine run better. Its value is in helping to alleviate trace detonation.

Harmful Detonation and Preignition

You can recognize abnormal detonation or preignition as follows (both have similar symptoms and consequences, but different causes):

- The knock is constant as the vehicle is cruising, climbing a slight grade, or gradually accelerating.
- The knock is severe, but tapers off as the vehicle accelerates.
- The knock is heard only as the vehicle coasts down.

Pinpointing the reason for an abnormal knock is difficult because there are many possible causes. Two conditions, carbon deposits in the engine and overheated spark plugs, cause preignition and should be rectified right away. Troubleshooting techniques for the other causes of detonation range from simple tests, such as checking the oil level, to complex procedures, such as testing computerized engine-control systems.

In the "Causes and Cures" table that follows, checking for preignition conditions is described first, because of the urgency for repair if engine damage is to be avoided. After preignition, the reasons for abnormal detonation are presented in approximate order of simplicity of repair, from less to more complex.

Causes and Cures: Preignition and Abnormal Detonation

Condition	What to Do
Preignition due to over-heating of spark plugs	Remove plugs and examine their tips. If they are white or blistered, replace the plugs with a colder set. Colder plugs, which dissipate heat rapidly, are especially suited for vehicles driven mainly at higher speeds, rather than in the city. Use the spark-plug manufacturer's reference chart (available at an auto parts and accessories store) to identify the designation of the spark plug that is *one* step colder on the heat-range scale than the spark plugs that have been in use. Install a set of colder plugs.
Preignition due to deposits inside the engine	Use an engine carbon-deposit solvent. If the recommended number of treatments fails to relieve the knock, it's likely that the engine has a detonation and not preignition problem.
Detonation due to a vehicle design factor	Call a dealer and ask whether a technical service bulletin involving spark knock has been issued by the manufacturer. If the condition results from the failure of an emissions-control component, by law an emissions-control system must be covered by a five-year or 50,000-mile warranty. You can also get information about manufacturer's service bulletins by writing to the Center for Auto Safety, 2001 S Street N.W., Suite 410, Washington, D.C. 20009. List the make, model, and year of your car. Ask for information about engine knock, or describe any other problem you're having with your car. Enclose a self-addressed, business-sized envelope with 45 cents postage and allow 4 to 6 weeks for delivery.
Detonation due to excessive oil foaming	Check the oil level when the engine is cold. If it is above the Full mark on the dipstick, drain the excess oil.
Detonation because a high-voltage cable lies too close to a ground or too close to another cable	Check that no spark-plug cable rests on or near an engine bolt. If the engine has a computer control system with electronic spark timing, make certain that its cable harness isn't near a spark-plug cable or alternator wire. Make sure each spark-plug cable is secured in its designated position in the spark-plug cable harness. By doing so, you will assure that each cable is routed properly and is away from parts that could be causing electrical grounding. A grounded ignition circuit can alter timing and cause detonation.

Condition	What to Do
Detonation due to an inoperative thermostatic air-cleaner valve that traps hot air in the engine	Remove the duct from the carburetor snorkel. Start the engine, which should be cold, and look inside the snorkel to see whether the air door moves to close off the hot-air opening from the exhaust manifold and then opens as the engine warms up (see page 37). Replace a damaged duct, hose, air-door motor, thermal-vacuum switch, or air door.
Detonation because a stuck manifold heat-control valve traps hot air in the engine	With the engine cold, check whether you can move the heat-control valve in the exhaust manifold. Push on the counterweight—an external part that is connected by a shaft to the heat-control valve inside the exhaust manifold—to see if it moves freely. If it doesn't, lubricate the accessible part of the shaft with heat-control-valve lubricant. Tap the counterweight lightly from side to side using a small hammer. If several treatments don't free the valve, the exhaust manifold may have to be replaced (see page 66). *Note:* On some cars a vacuum valve and thermal-vacuum switch regulate the heat-control valve. With the engine running, pull the hose off the vacuum valve and hold your finger over the end of the hose. Lack of suction indicates a damaged hose or thermal-vacuum switch. Inspect the hose, then test the vacuum valve with a hand-held vacuum pump, following the instructions provided with the hand-held vacuum pump.
Detonation due to faulty ignition timing	Use a timing light and tachometer to check ignition timing to the specification provided in the manufacturer's repair manual. At the same time check vacuum-advance and centrifugal-advance performance. If you find that timing is correct and advance mechanisms are in good condition, retard timing two degrees at a time to see whether the knock dissipates. You can safely retard timing a total of six degrees from specification. In many cases, doing this will get rid of abnormal detonation.
Detonation because of an inoperative EGR system	Warm up the engine. Put on a work glove and reach under the EGR valve to see whether you can feel the valve diaphragm (see page 36). In most cars, the valve diaphragm is exposed. Open and close the throttle. You should feel the diaphragm moving. If the diaphragm is sealed, use instructions in the manufacturer's service manual to test it, or have a mechanic determine whether the EGR system is activated when exhaust backpressure is present (positive backpressure) or absent (negative backpressure). The type

Condition	What to Do
	of system depends on the make and year of the car and the type of engine. Repair-manual instructions must then be followed to test the system. Replace a faulty EGR valve.
Detonation because an air leak where the carburetor and intake manifold join is producing a lean fuel mixture	Connect a vacuum gauge to a vacuum fitting on the carburetor or intake manifold and run the engine at idle speed. A vacuum-gauge reading that's below normal, but holds steady, indicates an air leak. A normal reading is generally 17 to 21 inches of mercury, but some engines have a normal reading lower than this; check the repair manual. To verify the existence of an air leak, squirt engine oil around the carburetor and intake manifold joint. If there is a leak, the vacuum-gauge reading will rise momentarily. Tighten carburetor bolts as much as possible. If tightening doesn't seal the leak, take the carburetor off and replace the gasket between the carburetor and intake manifold.
Detonation due to a bad head gasket, causing abnormally high cylinder pressure	Connect a vacuum gauge to a vacuum fitting on the carburetor or intake manifold, and run the engine at different speeds. A vacuum-gauge needle that flutters over a range of about 10 inches of mercury at all speeds indicates a bad head gasket. Replace it. If you don't have the repair manual, which describes how to replace a head gasket, the job should be done by a professional mechanic.
Detonation caused by a restricted exhaust system	Connect a vacuum gauge to a vacuum fitting on the carburetor or intake manifold, and accelerate the engine. If the gauge needle dips from a normal reading to near zero and then begins to rise again, the exhaust system is blocked. Look for mud clogging the tailpipe; then, for a crushed exhaust system part. Replace any damaged parts.
Detonation due to engine overheating	A dashboard temperature gauge or glowing warning light indicates overheating and possibly coolant loss. Tune up the cooling system by testing the radiator cap, checking for coolant leaks, tightening the drive belt, draining and flushing the cooling system, and making sure the fan is working (see chapter 11).
Detonation caused by failure of a computerized engine-control sensor	If you don't have the manufacturer's service manual, have a mechanic use an ohmmeter to find the faulty sensor. Possible culprits include the manifold absolute-pressure sensor, differential-pressure sensor, barometric-pressure sensor, vehicle-speed sensor, or throttle-position sensor. A faulty sensor should be replaced.

7

Hesitation and Stalling

TROUBLESHOOTING BRIEF

A hesitation as you attempt to accelerate your car can be annoying. If, as often happens, hesitation culminates in a stall, the condition could be a safety hazard.

The reason for hesitation and stalling is usually confined to one of six systems: accelerator-pump inside the carburetor, automatic choke, thermostatic air-cleaner, exhaust-gas-recirculation (EGR), exhaust manifold heat-control, and ignition-timing device and distributor-advance. Many of the system tests are made by simply observing what is or isn't happening.

PROJECT DATA

Special tools and materials. Manufacturer's repair manual, carburetor-and-choke cleaner, tachometer, heat-control-valve solvent, timing light.

Possible replacement parts. Accelerator pump, vacuum hose, air cleaner, air duct, EGR valve, distributor vacuum-advance unit.

Tasks that require two people. Testing the accelerator-pump system, choke system, thermostatic air-cleaner, EGR system, and exhaust manifold heat-control system.

Job difficulty and time. Degree of difficulty is relative to the mechanic's experience; all times are approximate.

- Testing accelerator-pump system: Easy, 15 minutes.
- Testing choke system: Easy, 10–20 minutes.
- Cleaning choke system: Easy, 10 minutes.
- Replacing choke vacuum-break: Moderately difficult, 45 minutes.
- Testing and setting fast-idle speed: Moderately difficult, 20–30 minutes.
- Testing thermostatic air cleaner: Easy, 20 minutes.
- Testing EGR system: Easy to moderately difficult, depending on the type of EGR valve, 10–30 minutes.
- Replacing EGR valve: Easy, 15–30 minutes.
- Testing exhaust manifold heat-control system: Easy, 10 minutes.
- Lubricating exhaust manifold heat-control valve shaft: Easy, 10 minutes.
- Checking ignition timing and distributor-advance units: Moderately difficult, 30 minutes.

Safety precautions. Fuel and fuel vapors, and the hydrogen gas given off by car batteries, ignite easily and explosively. When working on a car, never smoke or bring a device that can create sparks near the car.

- Work outdoors, not in an enclosed space, and always keep a dry chemical (class B) fire extinguisher nearby.
- To prevent electrical sparks, disconnect the negative battery terminal when performing any test that does not require you to crank the engine.
- Watch out for pulleys and belts when the engine is running; never wear loose clothing, watches, rings, or other jewelry when working on a car.

Hesitation *aka* Stumble

Hesitation on acceleration and the stalling that sometimes accompanies it are common problems that can usually be traced to a malfunctioning accelerator pump, choke, thermostatic air cleaner, exhaust gas recirculation, exhaust manifold heat-control, or ignition-timing and distributor-advance systems.

The Accelerator Pump

The accelerator-pump system is used only in carburetors. Therefore, this portion of the chapter does not apply to engines equipped with electronic fuel injection.

When you press the gas pedal to accelerate, the carburetor accelerator pump should squirt fuel into each primary carburetor throat. (A throat is also called a barrel.) If this doesn't happen, stumbling will result.

To check the accelerator pump, remove the top of the air cleaner and look down into the carburetor throat. If the engine is cold, push open the choke plate so you can see into the throat. Have a helper press the gas pedal to the floor. Each time the pedal is pressed, you should see a strong stream of fuel squirt into each of the carburetor's primary throats.

In a single-barrel carburetor, the primary throat is the single barrel. In two-barrel carburetors, if both barrels are of the same diameter, then each barrel is a primary throat. Fuel should squirt into each barrel when the accelerator pedal is depressed. On some two-barrel carburetors, one throat is larger in diameter than the other. The smaller barrel is primary, and the larger barrel is secondary; fuel should squirt only into the primary barrel. In a four-barrel carburetor, the primary throats are the two smaller-diameter barrels.

If an accelerator pump does not deliver a strong fuel stream to the primary throat or throats, the accelerator-pump system needs repair. An accelerator pump will fail to work properly when the pump plunger becomes worn, brittle, or cracked, or when the accelerator-pump check valve malfunctions, which is usually caused by dirt blocking the check-valve orifice. The carburetor must be removed and disassembled to work on the accelerator pump system. Leave the job to a professional mechanic if you do not have the experience, necessary tools, and instructions given in the manufacturer's manual.

The Choke

The choke system is also used only with carburetors; therefore, this portion of the chapter does not apply to engines equipped with electronic fuel injection.

A choke that malfunctions when the engine is cold can cause the engine to hesitate and stall during acceleration. To check the choke system, the engine should be cold. Remove the air cleaner. Hold the throttle half open. With your other hand, move the choke plate through its complete range of motion. It should not bind. If it does, find out why. A warped carburetor air horn, caused by overtightening the air cleaner, or a binding choke linkage or choke pivot are likely causes.

Liberal doses of choke cleaner sprayed on bound choke and choke-linkage pivots usually free them. If the carburetor air horn (opening) is warped a new carburetor is needed—an expensive repair. You can prevent this problem by tightening the air-cleaner hold-down fasteners snugly, but without excessive force.

To continue checking the choke system, hold the throttle half open and move the choke plate from its fully closed position. As you do this, watch the fast-idle cam (Figure 7-1). As the choke plate opens, the fast-idle cam should move. By the time the choke plate is vertical, the fast-idle cam should have dropped to where it can't touch the fast-idle screw on the throttle linkage when the throttle is released. If the fast-idle mechanism doesn't work, a dirty linkage is usually the reason. Use choke cleaner as described by instructions on the product's label to clean the fast-idle cam and linkage.

There is yet another test of the choke system to make. (Caution: Make sure the transmission is in Park or Neutral and the parking brake is engaged.) The car should be parked on level ground, not on a slope. To trip the choke and set it in the fully closed position, have someone in the car press the accelerator pedal to the floor once and release it. Then have your assistant start the engine while you watch the choke plate.

When the engine starts, the choke vacuum-break should immediately cause the choke plate to open slightly. (Other terms for the choke vacuum-break are choke vacuum kick and choke unloader.) If the plate remains

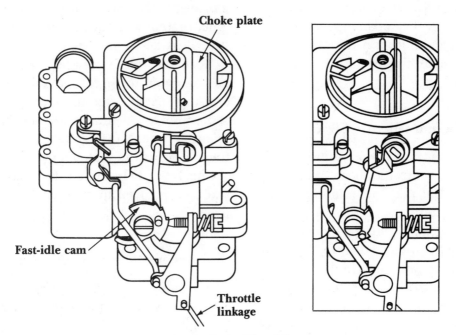

Figure 7–1   Fast-idle cam

completely closed, check to be sure the vacuum hose is connected to the choke vacuum-break.

If the hose is secured, pull the hose from the choke unloader and place your finger over the end of the hose to see if a vacuum pull (suction) is present. If so, the choke unloader is getting vacuum. Therefore, the part itself must be faulty and should be replaced. If you don't have experience, the right tools, and a repair manual, leave this job to a mechanic.

If no vacuum is present at the end of the hose, however, trace the hose to the vacuum port on the engine. A bent hose or a split hose will prevent vacuum from reaching the vacuum-break. Also, make certain the hose is connected to its vacuum port.

Some carburetors have two choke vacuum-breaks—a primary and a secondary. The choke plate should still open slightly when the cold engine is started. If it doesn't, check both vacuum-breaks and their hoses.

Watch the choke plate while the engine

idles. As the engine warms up, the plate should open gradually until it is wide open. If the choke binds, use choke cleaner to try to free it. If cleaner doesn't work, the choke should be overhauled by a professional mechanic.

Use a tachometer to check fast-idle speed (or cold-idle speed). Follow instructions that come with the tachometer. Generally, you attach the power (hot) lead of the instrument to the terminal of the ignition coil that supports the primary wire. The primary wire runs to the distributor. Then attach the ground lead of the tachometer to a clean metal part of the engine.

Be sure the engine is cold. Start it up and see if the tachometer records the specified fast-idle speed. The specification is often printed on the tune-up specification decal in the engine compartment. If not, it's in the manufacturer's repair manual for your car. If the fast-idle speed is too low, a cold engine can stumble when you put the car in gear. The fast-idle speed is usually set by turning the fast-idle screw against the fast-idle cam. (Check the repair manual to determine whether there is a deviation from this procedure.) Both parts are attached to the carburetor.

The Thermostatic Air-Cleaner

The thermostatic air-cleaner is used with carburetors and throttle body electronic fuel injection, but not with multiport electronic fuel injection.

When the engine is cold, the thermostatic air-cleaner allows preheated air to be drawn through the carburetor or throttle body and into the intake manifold. Heated air helps vaporize the atomized fuel from the carburetor or throttle body; without it, the gas would tend to condense before it reached the combustion chambers. If the thermostatic air-cleaner malfunctions and cold air is drawn in during engine warm-up, the car can stumble during acceleration, and may stall.

Check the thermostatic air-cleaner system by following the procedure given in chapter 4, "Emissions-Control Systems," starting on page 37.

Exhaust Gas Recirculation

The exhaust-gas-recirculation (EGR) system is used with carburetors, throttle body electronic fuel injection, and most multiport electronic fuel-injection systems. For multiport electronic fuel injection, refer to a repair manual to determine if the engine has an EGR system.

Oxides of nitrogen, which are air pollutants, form when high temperature causes nitrogen and oxygen to combine. The EGR system keeps oxides of nitrogen emissions at an acceptable level by recirculating exhaust gas through the intake manifold and into the combustion chambers. The exhaust

gas lowers the temperature inside the engine, thereby helping to curtail the formation of oxides of nitrogen.

Normally, the EGR system allows exhaust gas to enter the intake manifold only at cruising speeds after the engine is hot. It should never let exhaust gas into the intake manifold when the engine is cold. If it does, the engine will hesitate and probably stall.

Check the EGR system by following the procedures given in chapter 4, starting on page 36.

Exhaust Manifold Heat Control

The exhaust manifold heat-control system is used only on engines equipped with carburetors.

The exhaust manifold heat-control system diverts hot exhaust gas from the exhaust manifold to the intake manifold. Air mixes with the exhaust gas to make a fuel mixture that ignites and burns better while the engine is still cold, thus preventing hesitation on acceleration and a possible stall.

The heat-control system uses a valve called the heat-riser or manifold heat-control valve to pass hot air to the intake manifold. When the engine warms up and heats air by itself, the valve opens to allow exhaust gas to pass out through the exhaust system. If the valve should remain closed, the engine would overheat. Detonation (see chapter 6) and possibly a loss of power would result.

Two methods are commonly used to operate heat-riser valves: a bimetal spring that expands and contracts with changes in temperature, or a vacuum device.

Bimetal Spring   To check a valve with a bimetal spring, the engine must be cold. Reach down and grasp the valve's counterweight, which is attached to the exhaust manifold. You should be able to rotate it back and forth. If it's stuck, try to free it by spraying heat-control-valve solvent around the area where the counterweight shaft pivots. Then tap the shaft—*not the counterweight*—a few times with a ball-peen hammer. Repeat the procedure until the valve loosens and can be rotated. If the procedure doesn't work, the exhaust manifold, which houses the valve, will probably have to be replaced.

Vacuum Actuator To check a vacuum-controlled heat-riser valve, the engine must be cold. When a cold engine is started, a thermal sensor allows vacuum to pass to the heat-riser valve's vacuum actuator. The sensor is usually located in the air cleaner, where it senses air temperature, or is screwed into the engine or radiator, where it senses coolant temperature. As the engine warms up, the sensor reduces the vacuum to the vacuum actuator and the heat-riser valve gradually closes.

Make sure the vacuum hose that connects to the valve actuator is in good condition and tightly connected at each end (see Figure 7-2). Have someone start the engine as you watch the rod that extends from the vacuum diaphragm to the valve shaft. You should see this actuating rod move.

If it doesn't move, turn off the engine and clean the rod with carburetor-and-choke cleaner, then do the test again. If the rod still doesn't move, disconnect the rod and unbolt the vacuum diaphragm from its bracket. Replace the defective vacuum diaphragm.

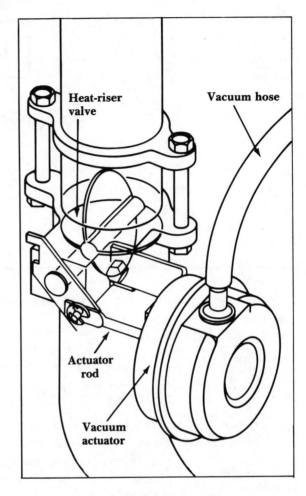

Figure 7–2 Vacuum actuator

is running at the idling speed specified in the repair manual. Adjust timing to specification, if necessary.

The timing procedure varies from car to car, so you will have to use both the instructions outlined in the repair manual and those that accompany the timing light itself. These instructions will also describe how to determine if the spark and centrifugal advance units are working properly.

Note: Engines equipped with nonelectronically controlled carburetors have distributors that contain spark and centrifugal advance units. Engines equipped with electronically controlled carburetors or electronic fuel-injection systems do not have these units.

Ignition Timing and Distributor Advance

Incorrect ignition timing can cause hesitation during acceleration. To check ignition timing, the engine should be warmed up. Disconnect and plug the vacuum hose at the distributor vacuum-advance unit. Check timing with a timing light while the engine

8

Rough Idle

TROUBLESHOOTING BRIEF

Do not ignore rough idling. It is a sign that the fuel mixture in one or more cylinders is not igniting. The fault often lies with a fuel mixture that is too rich with gasoline or too lean because of too much air. An overly rich or lean mixture usually results from deficient fuel-delivery or from an air leak in the fuel-delivery system. It can also be caused by an engine malfunction, such as a loss of vacuum because of a cracked hose or damaged valve.

But fuel-system or engine malfunctions aren't the only reasons for rough idle. Quite often, the problem lies in the ignition system. Whatever the cause, you should track it down. Fixing it will improve driving comfort and contribute to fuel economy. One dead cylinder in a four-cylinder engine, for example, will waste 25 percent of the gas you buy.

Looking and listening inspections will usually reveal the cause of rough idle. If they fail to uncover the reason for the condition, testing with a tachometer and a compression gauge is called for.

PROJECT DATA

Special tools and materials. Manufacturer's repair manual, plastic or rubber hammer, torque wrench, mechanic's stethoscope, tachometer, timing light, spark-plug cable pliers, carburetor-and-choke cleaner, compression gauge.

Possible replacement parts. Vacuum hose, carburetor air filter, ignition coil, spark-plug cables, distributor cap, distributor, valve cover gasket, intake manifold gasket.

Job difficulty and time. Degree of difficulty is relative to the mechanic's experience; all times are approximate.

- Inspecting carburetor air filter: Easy, 5 minutes.
- Inspecting carburetor: Easy, 5 minutes.
- Checking air and vacuum hoses: Easy, 20–30 minutes.
- Tracking down a noisy component: Easy, 15 minutes.
- Testing and adjusting slow-idle (or curb-idle) speed: Easy, 15 minutes.
- Testing fast-idle speed: Moderately difficult, 20 minutes.
- Testing for an air leak: Easy, 15 minutes.
- Testing engine compression: Easy to moderately difficult, depending on the engine, 30–60 minutes.

Safety precautions. Fuel and fuel vapors, and the hydrogen gas given off by car batteries, ignite easily and explosively. When working on a car, never smoke or bring a device that can create sparks near the car.

- Work outdoors, not in an enclosed space, and always keep a dry chemical (class B) fire extinguisher nearby.
- To prevent electrical sparks, disconnect the negative battery terminal when performing any test that does not require you to crank the engine.
- Watch out for pulleys and belts when the engine is running; never wear loose clothing, watches, rings, or other jewelry when working on a car.

Looking and Listening Inspections

Simply reconnecting a loose ignition cable or vacuum hose can often eliminate rough idle. To begin troubleshooting, check each spark-plug cable at both ends to ensure that cables are tightly connected. A disconnected or loose cable will prevent spark from reaching and igniting the fuel mixture in the cylinder. Follow this by inspecting each vacuum and air hose from end to end. A loose or cracked hose can cause hesitation and stalling (see chapter 7) as well as rough idle.

Bear in mind that vacuum hoses attach to components that require vacuum (or suction) created by the engine in order to function. There may be a placard inside the engine compartment that shows the routing of each hose and to which component it connects. If this placard is missing or obliterated, consult the manufacturer's repair manual. Check all vacuum hoses for cracks and make certain all hose connections are tight. Replace damaged hoses and tighten loose connections as necessary. To test for clogged hoses or hidden hose leaks, you must disconnect each hose at the component end and hold your finger over the hose's end with the engine running. If you feel suction, the hose is fine. Also check the vacuum port on the intake manifold or carburetor to make certain it's unobstructed.

Now remove the air cleaner and examine the air filter serving the carburetor or fuel injection system. If the air filter is dirty, replace it. A dirty filter blocks air which makes the fuel mixture too rich.

Examine the carburetor. (Note: This procedure does not apply if the engine is equipped with a fuel-injection system.) If the outside of the carburetor is wet with gas, it's a sign that the float-and-needle valve assembly is worn, or that a piece of dirt has lodged between the needle and its seat. Either problem will cause excess gas to flow into the carburetor, and make the fuel mixture too rich. Gas will also overflow the carburetor and leak out.

Tap the carburetor bowl near the fuel-line connection with a plastic or rubber hammer. This may dislodge any dirt and stop the flooding. If not, or if the float needle or

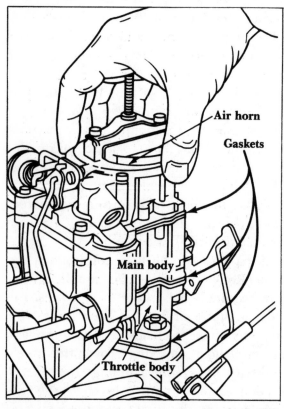

Movement at any of the points indicated by the arrows means that the fasteners are loose and need tightening. The illustration shows a carburetor, but you can use it as a guide to check a throttle body.

Figure 8–1 Grasping the carburetor

its seat is damaged, the carburetor must be overhauled by a professional mechanic, unless you have the experience, special tools, and instructions needed to do the job.

Next, grasp the carburetor or throttle body of a throttle-body fuel-injection system by the top of the air horn. The air horn of the carburetor or throttle body contains the choke plate or fuel injector, respectively, (Note: This procedure does not apply if the engine is equipped with multiport fuel injection.) Try to rock the carburetor or throttle body back and forth (see Figure 8-1). If it moves, leaks around the gaskets are allowing air into the intake manifold, leaning out the fuel mixture and causing rough idle. Use a torque wrench to tighten to specification the bolts that attach the carburetor or throttle body to the intake manifold.

Further Checks Listen for any unusual sounds while the engine idles. For example, high-voltage sparks jumping to ground from a defective spark-plug cable or cracked ignition coil or distributor cap can make a sharp cracking noise. Inspect spark-plug cables for brittle insulation and cracks, and check the coil and distributor cap for cracks (see Figure 8-2). A bad ignition coil cannot be repaired so you must replace it. A damaged distributor cap must also be replaced. In addition, check for split, oil-soaked, or brittle spark-plug boots. If you find one, replace it. Replacement boots are available for some engines. Others have boots molded to cables; the cable has to be replaced.

A more conclusive examination to find a faulty ignition component can be made by examining ignition components in the dark with the engine running. If you see flashes of electricity from the ignition coil, a spark-plug cable, or distributor cap, it indicates that the part is defective and should be replaced.

You may hear a hissing or whistling sound

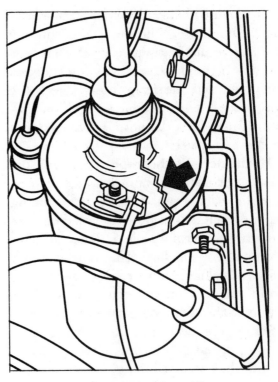

Cracked ignition coil

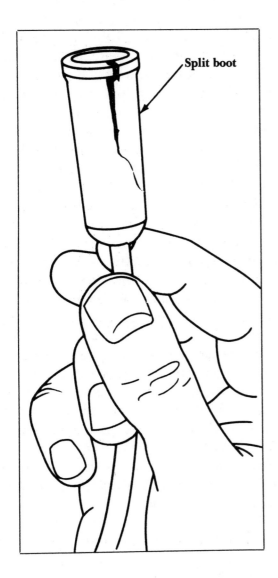

Split boot

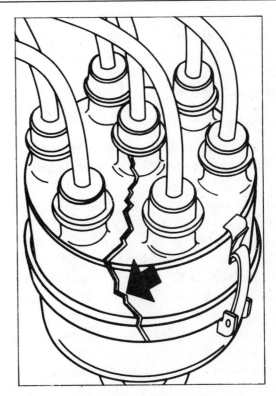

Cracked distributor cap

Figure 8–2   Some causes of sharp cracking noises

as the engine idles, which is a sign of a leaking vacuum hose. With the engine running at idle, use pliers to squeeze off each hose in turn. If the noise ceases as you squeeze, you've located the leaky hose. Check the hose to see if it is connected securely on each end. If it is, then the hose is damaged and should be replaced.

Mechanic's Stethoscope Any unusual metallic or slapping noise may be coming from the valve train, distributor, or timing chain or belt. Damage to any of these systems can cause rough idle. Using a mechanic's stethoscope makes verification a simpler matter. Its long, thin probe allows you to worm the tool on to parts that lie deep within the engine compartment. Caution: Keep fingers away from the moving parts as you put the stethoscope probe in place.

With the engine running, place the stethoscope probe on each area of the engine. Start at the front of the engine at the timing chain or belt cover. Then, listen at the distributor, and finally at the engine itself. When listening for noise from inside the engine, place the probe on the valve cover above each spark plug. If there is a noisy component inside the engine, the stethoscope will help you hear it.

Noise from inside the timing chain or belt cover usually means that a loose chain or belt is slapping against the cover. This alters valve timing, causing the engine to idle roughly. The timing chain or belt will probably have to be replaced, but first determine if there is an adjustment that can be made. Special tools and a repair manual are needed to make an adjustment or to replace the chain or belt, so you may want to leave those jobs to a professional mechanic.

A bad timing chain or belt can also be identified by using a timing light aimed at the timing pulley. If the timing marks appear to "jump" around, the chain or belt may be bad. Manufacturers recommend regular inspection and replacement of timing belts; chains wear in time, but do not require regular maintenance.

Noise from inside the distributor usually comes from a worn distributor shaft. A worn shaft alters ignition timing, or causes the rotor to hit the distributor cap or the reluctor to hit the pickup coil. All these events affect the delivery of spark to one or more cylinders, thereby causing rough idle. Remove the distributor cap and see if you can wiggle the distributor shaft from side to side. Movement means the distributor should be replaced.

Valve Problems A heavy metallic noise from inside the engine at one or more plugs indicates a bad valve lifter, push rod, rocker arm, or valve spring. Any of these prevents the proper valve operation necessary for the engine to run smoothly. Remove the valve cover—it's held in place with bolts—and discard the gasket. Bear in mind: You have to install a new gasket when reinstalling the cover to ensure that the cover is properly sealed. Installing a valve cover is a moderately difficult and time consuming job.

Start the engine and allow it to run at idle. Watch the rocker arms (see Figure 8-3). Each should move the same amount. If you see one that barely moves, remains still, or gyrates rather than moving smoothly, the valve operated by that rocker arm is causing trouble. The cylinder head should be taken off to examine the valve system more closely. If you haven't had experience in doing engine work of this sort, let a professional mechanic take over.

Instrument Tests

If a visual and listening inspection fails to turn up the reasons for rough idle, the cause can be pinpointed by using a compression gauge and tachometer.

Compression Gauge Take a compression reading from each cylinder (see page 50) and compare the readings with manufacturer specifications given in the repair manual. A low reading in a cylinder could mean you have a burned valve, which cannot seat itself against the cylinder head. This causes a loss of compression that leads to a loss of power, characterized by rough idle and running. To make sure, squirt a teaspoonful of motor oil into the cylinder that gives the low reading and take another reading. If the reading remains the same, a burned valve is the problem. If cylinder compression rises, you may have worn piston rings. In any case, have a professional mechanic take over troubleshooting and repair.

Tachometer Instructions on how to connect a tachometer (or tach) accompany the instrument. They call for attaching the positive (hot) lead to the side terminal of the ignition coil that supports the primary wire from the distributor, and connecting the negative lead to a clean ground on the engine.

Check slow-idle (or curb-idle) speed, but first warm up the engine. If the tach indicates that slow idle revolutions per minute (rpm) is not at the specification given in the repair manual, make the adjustment as spelled out in that manual. Be sure you consult the correct section of the manual—the section that applies to carburetors or to electronic fuel injection, whichever your engine has.

Use your tachometer to perform a power-balance test. You will also need spark-plug cable pliers. The power-balance test involves interrupting spark to each cylinder while watching the tach to see how much of a drop there is in engine rpm. There should be a sharp drop. Furthermore, the drop for all cylinders as recorded by the tachometer should be about the same. If the rpm drop is slight or there is no drop, the particular

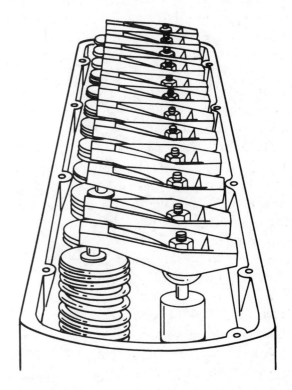

Figure 8–3 Rocker arms with valve covers removed

cylinder being tested isn't performing properly and is the reason for the engine idling roughly.

To do the power-balance test, connect the tach and have the engine running at idle. Use your spark-plug cable pliers to remove cables from spark plugs one at a time as you watch the tachometer to note the reading to which the rpm drops. Write down the reading and reattach the cable. Wait a few seconds before pulling off the next cable.

When all readings have been taken, compare them. If the test reveals a weak cylinder—one that doesn't cause a drop in engine speed—you must determine if the reason is a fuel or ignition system problem (see chapters 1 and 2). If it is neither, then there is a malfunction inside the engine with that cylinder; the repair job should be left to a professional mechanic.

If the cause of rough idle hasn't yet been

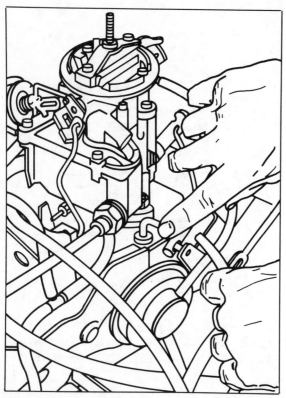

Figure 8–4 Checking for vacuum at the intake manifold

fuel-enrichment test. This will establish whether there is an air leak into the fuel-delivery system that escaped your visual inspection.

With the engine idling, spray carburetor-and-choke cleaner along the joint at the base of the carburetor or throttle body, around air ducts of carburetor or fuel injection systems, and around the mass air-flow sensor of a multiport fuel-injection system. If the tachometer shows an increase in speed and the engine begins to run smoothly, it confirms that an air leak at the point being sprayed is causing a lean fuel mixture. Replace the part or tighten bolts, whichever is necessary to seal the area.

Finally, use the tachometer to check each vacuum hose. Start where the hose is attached to the vacuum port on the carburetor, throttle body, or intake manifold. Disconnect each hose, in turn, and plug the vacuum port (see Figure 8-4). If the tachometer shows an increase in engine speed and the idle smooths out, the vacuum hose or the component it attaches to is leaking. Replace the hose. If that doesn't help, replace the component.

uncovered, keep the tachometer connected to the engine and use a can of carburetor-and-choke cleaner to perform an artificial

9

Low Gas Mileage

MAINTENANCE BRIEF

Even when your car runs smoothly without skipping a beat, it may not be working as efficiently and economically as it should. Fuel economy declines long before a car begins to show a reduction in performance. That's because there are a number of critical factors that affect engine efficiency.

Test Standards and Goals

To determine which maintenance factors are most important for keeping a car's fuel mileage up to par, a test car equipped with a miles-per-gallon gauge was driven 2,000 miles on roads in south Florida.

Ten separate test runs were conducted. Before tests were conducted, the engine and tires were examined carefully and adjusted to specification to assure that no hidden deficiency would have a bearing on baseline test results. The first test established a baseline: the maximum fuel economy of the test vehicle. The nine other test runs were done with intentionally created maintenance defects. Each test covered 200 miles. After each, the defect was corrected and another was introduced. The purpose of the tests was to determine how much fuel each minor problem steals from car owners.

The nine deficiencies introduced into the test car follow:

1. Ignition timing was retarded 6 degrees from specification.
2. Ignition timing was advanced 6 degrees from specification.
3. Spark-plug gaps were closed 0.02 inch from specification, to simulate fouled plugs.
4. Spark-plug gaps were opened 0.02 inch from specification, to simulate worn plugs.
5. Engine idle speed was increased 50 rpm from specification.
6. Tire pressure was reduced 8 pounds per square inch (psi) below the recommended maximum.
7. Tire pressure was increased 4 psi above recommended maximum.
8. The carburetor air filter was partially clogged.
9. A vacuum leak was simulated by disconnecting a vacuum hose.

The nine tests selected involve relatively minor maintenance defects, rather than serious problems that generally make fuel mileage drop dramatically. Major defects cause problems that car owners usually fix as soon as possible; they create performance flaws that car owners find hard to accept. Major problems include hard starting, stalling, missing, rough idling, hesitation, engine run-on (dieseling), black exhaust, engine knock, unsteady steering, and abnormal tire wear.

Test Methods

The test car was equipped with a 2.3-liter (140 cubic inch) four-cylinder engine, single-barrel carburetor, and three-speed automatic transmission.

A miles-per-gallon gauge was installed in the engine compartment (see Figure 9-1). The manufacturer of the gauge states that it's accurate to within ½ percent. The gauge was connected to the fuel line between the fuel pump and the carburetor, with an on-off switch mounted near the driver.

To operate the gauge the test driver pressed the switch, causing a red light to glow. At the same time he noted the odometer reading. When the red light went out, indicating that ¹⁄₁₀ gallon of gasoline had passed through the gauge, he again read the odometer. The difference between the two readings gave the distance traveled using ¹⁄₁₀ gallon of fuel. To calculate miles per gallon, the distance was multiplied by 10. Thus, if the car traveled 2.4 miles from light-on to light-off, the car was judged to be getting 24 mpg.

To measure fuel consumption more precisely, a simple gauge was devised to make it easy to read the odometer. The gauge—three equidistant lines drawn on an adhe-

Figure 9–1 Miles-per-gallon gauge installed in the engine compartment

sive label that was pressed onto the dash in line with the odometer face—divided the odometer's ¹⁄₁₀-mile digits into one-quarter, one-half, and three-quarter increments. This allowed the test driver to get readings in quarter multiples, for example, 25.25 mpg, 18.5 mpg, 23.75 mpg, and so on.

To minimize uncontrollable variables that could have affected accuracy, tests were run on the same roads and the same brand of gas was purchased from the same station. The same number of readings were made for each test. At the end of each test, readings were averaged.

Results

With the engine and tires adjusted to manufacturer specifications and without any defects induced, the car averaged 25.75 mpg. The table "Changes in Gas Mileage Caused by Maintenance Defects" shows test results when each of the nine deficiencies listed at the beginning of this chapter was induced.

Summary and Conclusions

Tests indicate that mistimed ignition and improperly gapped or defective spark plugs cause a significant decrease in miles per gallon. By contrast, the other alterations to the test car, except for one, showed only minor losses in fuel economy. The one exception—

Changes in Gas Mileage Caused by Maintenance Defects			
Condition	Average reading (mpg)*	Variation from baseline (mpg)*	Percentage decrease (−) or increase (+) from baseline
Car in perfect condition (baseline)	25.75 mpg	—	—
Timing retarded 6 degrees	22.00	−3.75 mpg	−14.0%
Timing advanced 6 degrees	21.00	−4.75	−18.0
Spark-plug gap closed 0.02 inch	20.75	−5.00	−19.0
Spark-plug gap opened 0.02 inch	19.25	−6.50	−25.0
Idle speed increased 50 rpm	24.50	−1.25	−2.0
Tire pressure decreased 8 psi	25.25	−0.50	−1.5
Tire pressure[1] increased 4 psi	26.50	+0.75	+3.0
Partially clogged air filter[2]	24.50	−1.25	−2.0
Vacuum hose disconnected	23.75	−2.0	−8.0

*Rounded off to the nearest 0.25 mile.

[1]Tire pressure was increased to 39 psi, which was 10.3 percent more than the maximum specification (35 psi) printed on the tire sidewalls. But you should never exceed specification. Doing so will lead to abnormal tire wear.
[2]The clogged air filter installed in the test car had been used in another car for 12,000 miles.

inflating tires above the recommended specification—resulted in an increased fuel efficiency. The increase was expected, because greater air pressure reduces the rolling resistance of tires, but overinflating tires will cause premature tire wear.

According to tests done in automotive laboratories, loss in fuel economy resulting from out-of-specification tune-up factors, such as worn spark plugs and incorrect ignition timing adjustments, have ranged from 9 to 12 percent. In the test car the loss ranged from 14 to 25 percent. The engines tested may explain the difference. In laboratory tests, six- and eight-cylinder engines are usually used. The test car used in Florida had a four-cylinder engine. A bad spark plug in a smaller engine wastes a greater percentage of fuel than one in a six- or eight-cylinder engine.

Differences in results aside, the major conclusion that can be drawn from fuel-economy testing follows: If you want to get maximum fuel economy, keep timing set to specification and keep spark plugs in mint condition. These factors should be checked every 12,000–15,000 miles. If your car is in poor condition, a tune-up and attention to any other defects will probably enable you to see a noticeable increase in miles per gallon. You may not notice improvement if your car has only one or two minor defects that don't have much effect on fuel economy, but it will occur.

Driving Habits That Yield Better Gas Mileage

Driving habits play a big role in the amount of fuel an engine uses. In a recent test, 20 identical cars were put into courier service. During the test they were periodically checked so that necessary adjustments and repairs could be made. All of the cars were driven daily under almost the same conditions until they reached approximately 100,000 miles. During the period, car-by-car mileage figures were taken by technicians to determine the miles per gallon attained by the different drivers.

According to test results, the miles per gallon over the entire testing period ranged from a high of about 33 to a low of about 26. The difference is attributable to driving habits. Those who weave in and out of traffic, make jack-rabbit starts, and slam on the brakes instead of coming to a gradual stop should consider their driving habits before complaining that their car is getting poor gas mileage.

The following summarizes sensible driving procedures that can help you attain maximum fuel economy:

- Observe the speed limit.
- Maintain a steady speed.
- Don't tailgate other vehicles and don't cut in and out of traffic.
- Anticipate stops. When approaching traffic lights, slow down by taking your foot off the accelerator. Let the car's rolling resistance help slow the car down before you apply the brakes to stop. Avoid racing up to red lights and heavy braking.
- In cold weather, try to keep the car warm by turning up the temperature and letting vents force heated air through the car rather than using the heater blower. The blower puts more load on the engine, thereby using more gas. If the blower is needed, keep it at the lowest setting you find comfortable.
- Shut off power-consuming accessories before you turn off the ignition, so the load on the engine is minimized the next time the engine is started.
- Don't race the engine just before turning off the ignition.
- Try to avoid idling the engine for more

than a minute. With the engine warm, it is more efficient to shut it off and restart it when you're ready to go.

- Avoid unnecessary steering wheel movement. Each sideward movement of the tires causes drag, which increases fuel consumption. When making turns, back off on the gas pedal and let the car slow down on its own. Touch the brake pedal lightly, if you have to. Try to lose all the speed you need to before you turn. Accelerate smoothly through the corner and back to cruising speed.

- Accelerate to speed as rapidly as necessary, but smoothly. Avoid "jackrabbit" starts.

- In cold weather, do not allow your car to warm up at idle for more than 30 seconds; your car will warm up quickly when driven.

- Accelerate slowly on sand and gravel, and on snowy, icy, or rain-slick roads. Avoid spinning the car's wheels.

- Anticipate hills. Gently press the gas pedal and maintain momentum to carry you over the hill top, but don't try to increase speed going uphill. Once over the crest, ease off on the gas pedal and let gravity help maintain car speed down the hill.

10

Overheating Engine

MAINTENANCE BRIEF

Internal-combustion engines cannot convert into power all the energy they produce by burning fuel. Only about one third of the energy, or heat, produced by an engine actually powers the car. Another third exits unutilized through the exhaust system. The rest must be dissipated into the air—the job of the cooling system. To perform its essential function well, the system must be clean, to permit the free flow of the liquid coolant, and tight, so it doesn't leak.

This chapter emphasizes maintenance, not troubleshooting. Maintenance helps prevent overheating. No automotive system lends itself better to preventive maintenance than the cooling system. But if the engine in your car should suddenly overheat, despite your efforts, the maintenance steps outlined in this chapter can be used as a troubleshooting guide.

PROJECT DATA

Special tools and materials. Manufacturer's repair manual, cooling system thermometer, cooling-system pressure tester, flushing T (or coolant flushing adapter), garden hose, hand-held vacuum pump.

Possible replacement parts. Thermostat, thermostat gasket, water-pump drive belt, radiator pressure cap.

Job difficulty and time. Degree of difficulty is relative to the mechanic's experience; all times are approximate.

- Cleaning debris from between radiator fins: Easy, 15 minutes.
- Testing the thermostat: Moderately difficult, 30 minutes.
- Testing fan clutch or electric fan: Easy, 15–30 minutes.
- Inspecting water-pump drive belt: Easy, 10 minutes.
- Replacing water-pump drive belt: Easy to moderately difficult, 15–30 minutes.
- Checking for leaks by pressure testing: Easy, 60 minutes.
- Testing radiator pressure cap: Easy, 10 minutes.
- Flushing cooling system: Easy, 30 minutes.

Safety precautions. Make sure the engine is *cold* when working on the cooling system unless the instructions given direct you to do otherwise.

- Beware of pulleys and belts when the engine is running; never wear loose clothing, watches, rings, or other jewelry when working on a car
- Never smoke or bring a device that creates sparks near the car. Fuel and fuel vapors, and the hydrogen gas given off by car batteries, ignite easily and explosively. Work outdoors, not in an enclosed space, and always keep a dry chemical (class B) fire extinguisher nearby.

The Cooling System

The cooling system removes heat from the engine by circulating a liquid coolant through passages surrounding the cylinders (combustion chambers). (See Figure 10-1.) Coolant absorbs heat from the engine. Hot coolant then circulates through the radiator, where heat is transferred from the coolant to the walls of the radiator core tubes. Heat passes into radiator fins that are bonded to the tubes. Air rushing over the fins as the car travels along and air directed over the radiator from a fan blows the heat from the fins into the atmosphere.

Every automobile radiator works the same way, but there are two types of radiator design: cross-flow and down-flow. In a down-flow radiator, hot coolant from the engine goes into a tank on top of the radiator core. The coolant flows down through tubes in the core, where it gives off heat. It then flows into a tank attached to the bottom of the core and back to the engine. In a cross-flow radiator, hot coolant flows into a tank situated on the side of the core, then across the radiator, where it gives off heat, and into another tank on the other side. Coolant is then pumped to the engine.

In either system, the tank that handles hot coolant has a filler neck equipped with a pressure cap. A spring-loaded valve in the cap is set to open at a preset pressure to prevent damage to the cooling system when high coolant temperature raises the system's internal pressure. The valve opens to vent the system. Pressure forces some coolant out of the radiator into a coolant recovery system, which in most cars consists of a hose that brings displaced coolant to a plastic reservoir. Without pressure venting, coolant would boil and the engine would overheat.

Both radiator designs use a fan. One type of fan is attached to the water-pump shaft and rotates as long as the engine is running. The other type operates electrically. When temperature exceeds a preset level at which coolant begins to boil, a thermostat closes to complete the circuit to the motor that powers the fan. Fans supply needed ventilation when the car is at a standstill or traveling at a slow speed and the flow of atmospheric air is curtailed.

The cooling system has a water pump and includes the heater. The water pump circulates coolant through the engine and cooling system. The heater, an often-overlooked part of the cooling system, is a small radiator. When the heater is on, hot coolant is pumped through the heater core and a blower fan forces the hot air into the passenger compartment. When the heater is off, the hot coolant bypasses the heater core through a bypass valve and circulates back to the radiator.

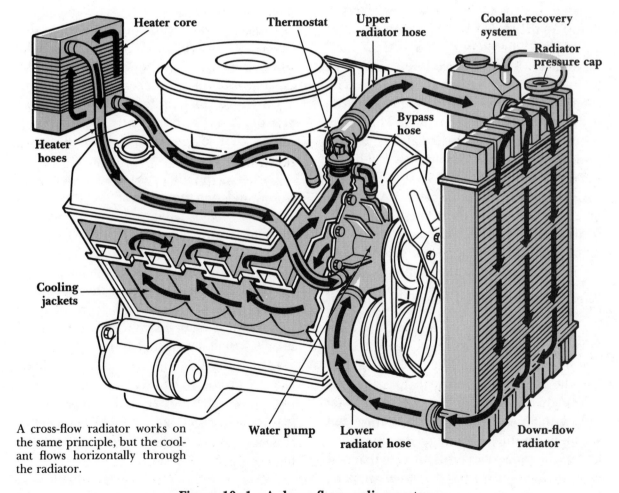

A cross-flow radiator works on the same principle, but the coolant flows horizontally through the radiator.

Figure 10–1   A down-flow cooling system

How to Prevent Overheating

Most of the following components should be inspected once a year to avoid a failure that can cause overheating and lead to an on-the-road breakdown.

Radiator Use compressed air or a soft brush to clean dead bugs and other debris from between the radiator fins. Inspect the radiator for spots of corrosion, which indicate small leaks. These leaks can get larger if they are not repaired. If you find a small corroded spot, try using a commercial radiator stop leak. If that doesn't work, have the leak repaired by a radiator service shop.

Radiator Pressure Cap With the engine cold, remove the radiator pressure cap and attach it to a cooling-system pressure tester. Pump up the tester until the gauge won't go any higher. The gauge should read the specification at which the cap is rated, usually 13 to 15 pounds per square foot. The specification may be embossed on the cap, or can be found in the repair manual. The gauge should hold the reading for at least 5 minutes. If not, replace the cap with one of the same design and with the same rating.

Cooling System Thermostat As the engine warms up, the thermostat should remain closed and block the flow of coolant to the radiator, thereby allowing hot coolant to circulate back into the engine and permitting the engine to warm up quickly. But the thermostat must open when the engine reaches normal operating temperature. If it fails to open, coolant cannot enter the radiator and cool down. The coolant will boil and the engine will overheat.

You do not have to test the thermostat unless the engine is overheating or not warming up quickly enough. If the engine is overheating—because the thermostat valve sticks in the closed position—the dashboard temperature gauge will rise or the warning light will come on. A dashboard temperature gauge will show a low reading if an engine is overcooling. In a car with a temperature warning light, failure of the heater to provide heat after the engine has been running for 5 minutes or longer indicates overcooling. Overcooling results when the thermostat valve sticks in the open position.

You need a cooling system thermometer, a pot filled with water, and the kitchen range to test a thermostat. Tie one end of a length of wire or string to the thermostat. Tie the other end of the wire or string to a wood dowel laid across the top of the pot. Place the thermostat in the water, but make sure it is suspended and not touching the sides or bottom of the pot.

Warm the water until the thermostat valve opens. Remove the pot from the range, take the thermostat from the water, and slip the end of a toothpick under the valve. Caution: Wear gloves to handle the thermostat, so you don't burn your hands. Let the thermostat cool so the valve closes and grasps the toothpick.

Immerse the thermostat in water once again, and put the pot back on the range. Heat the water using a low heat setting, holding the thermometer in the water, but away from the sides and bottom of the pan. When the thermostat valve opens enough to release the toothpick, read the thermometer. It should be within 10 degrees of the temperature stamped on the thermostat. If it isn't, install a new thermostat.

Important: Whether you install the old or a new thermostat, be sure to clean the metal parts of the thermostat housing with a wire brush. Use a new gasket to seal the joint where the two parts of the thermostat housing bolt together.

Fan Clutch Check the repair manual to determine whether the engine in your car is equipped with a fan clutch. On many belt-driven fans, a clutch allows the fan to free-wheel until the engine warms up. This prevents the fan from blowing cold air across the radiator when the engine has just been started, before it has warmed up. The fan clutch allows the engine to reach the normal operating temperature at which it runs most efficiently as quickly as possible. Conversely, if the fan clutch fails to engage when the engine does get warm, the fan won't rotate and the engine will overheat.

To test the fan clutch, make sure the engine is cold. Start it up and watch the fan, but keep a safe distance from belts, pulleys, and other moving parts. After the engine has been running for several minutes (wait a maximum of 10 minutes), you should see the fan begin to rotate. This means that the fan clutch has engaged the fan. If the fan does not begin to rotate within 10 minutes, have the fan clutch replaced.

Electric Fan   Many cars have electric fans controlled by a thermostatic switch (see Figure 10-2). The switch is usually screwed into the radiator tank and senses coolant temperature; it turns the fan on when the temperature reaches a preset level.

If your car has a thermostatically controlled electric fan, you can test it by driving the car until the engine is warmed up. Then park, turn off the engine, lift the hood, and look at the fan. It should be rotating, or begin to rotate in a few seconds. Caution: Keep your hands away from moving parts. A faulty temperature sensor is the most likely source of the problem; check the sensor and the leads running to it.

Water-Pump Drive Belt   Twist the drive belts of a belt-driven fan and examine them. The outside face may look healthy, but it could be hiding problems that an inspection of the underside can reveal (see Figure 10-3). If a belt is damaged, replace it as soon

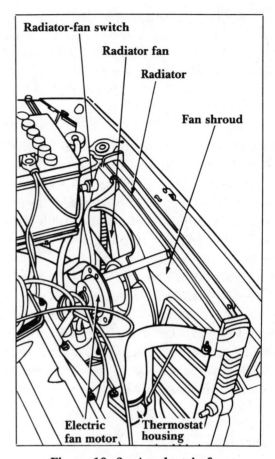

Figure 10-2   An electric fan

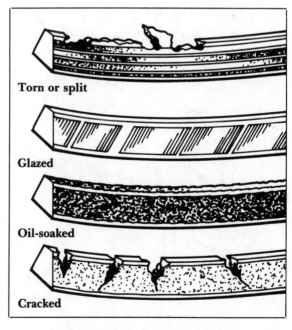

Figure 10-3   Damaged belts

as possible. If a belt snaps, the engine will overheat almost at once. Note: Use instructions provided in the repair manual to replace and adjust a drive belt.

Checking for Leaks

In addition to making the inspections given above, you should pressure-test the cooling system. A pressure test can help you find small leaks that could rupture suddenly and cause an abrupt loss of coolant. Such rapid coolant loss will cause the engine to overheat almost immediately.

The testing instrument, which is called a cooling-system pressure tester, allows you to place the cooling system under pressure equivalent to what it is subjected to when the car is being driven. A car's pressure specification is often stamped on the radiator cap, and always given in the repair man-

ual. With the system under pressure, radiator hoses, radiator, water pump, heater hoses, heater, and engine core plugs can be inspected for coolant leaks.

To pressurize the cooling system, make sure the engine is cold and turned off. Remove the cap from the radiator and attach the cooling-system pressure tester to the radiator filler neck (see Figure 10-4). Pump the tester until the gauge displays the maximum pressure for the cooling system.

Note: If you don't know the exact maximum pressure specification, pump the tester until it reads 15 pounds per square inch (psi), which is the pressure at which most cooling systems operate.

Make your way slowly around the engine. Look for a leak from radiator hoses, radiator, heater hoses, and heater. Make repairs as necessary.

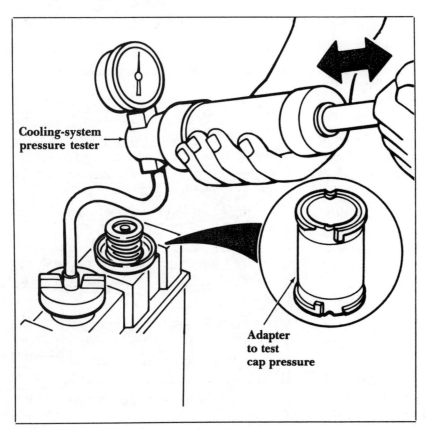

Cooling-system pressure tester

Adapter to test cap pressure

Figure 10–4 Using a cooling-system pressure tester

Parts That Need Extra Attention

A leak from the water pump and an engine core plug is often not apparent even with the system under pressure. Therefore, an extra step or two may be necessary.

Check the water pump after the parts mentioned above have been inspected. Disconnect the cooling-system pressure tester and replace the radiator cap. Start the engine and let it warm up about 5 minutes. Then turn the engine off, reconnect the pressure tester, and pump up pressure to specification. Observe the water pump as the engine cools down. Most pumps have a small vent hole on the underside of the housing, just below the pump shaft. A leaking water pump will force noticeable amounts of coolant out of this hole and leave traces of coolant under the car.

Engine core plugs are half-dollar-size discs driven into the side of the engine block at the base of the engine. Check core plugs last. Be sure the engine is cold, place the car on a lift or on jack stands, and see that the cooling-system pressure tester is still recording the specified maximum pressure.

Caution: Raise a car only on firm, level ground. If safety ramps are used, drive the car onto them. Place an automatic transmission in Park or a manual transmission in gear. Then turn off the engine and place chocks behind the rear wheels. If safety stands are used, set the transmission and use wheel chocks as above, then lift the front of the car high enough with a scissors jack to place stands under the left and right control arms. Slowly lower the car until it is supported by the safety stands. If the stands shift, raise the car and reposition the stands.

An engine generally has two core plugs on each side of the block. Corrosive (white) deposits, coolant around the spot where core plugs join the engine, or both are signs that plugs are leaking. If a core plug is leaking, have all the plugs replaced. When one has failed, it won't be long before they all fail.

Leaks Inside the Engine

If the cooling system is sound, pressure exerted on it by the cooling-system pressure tester—as recorded by the tester gauge—should be retained for an indefinite period. But if the gauge shows a drop in pressure after a few minutes, and the tests described above do not reveal an external leak, there could be a leak inside the engine. Coolant leaking through a cylinder-head gasket, cracked cylinder head, or cracked engine block often enters the engine lubricating system and mixes with oil. If you suspect an internal leak, perform the following test:

1. Start the engine and let it get hot.
2. Turn off the engine, open the hood, and pull the oil dipstick out of the dipstick tube. Caution: Keep your hands away from hot engine parts.
3. Allow a few drops of oil to drip from the dipstick onto the exhaust manifold, which will be extremely hot.

If you hear sizzling, it's likely that the engine has an internal crack. A professional mechanic will be able to verify this, probably using an exhaust-gas emissions analyzer to make a preliminary check.

An engine crack allows coolant to leak in one direction, into the lubricating system, and exhaust gas to leak in the opposite direction, into the cooling system. Using an exhaust-gas emissions analyzer (see Figure 10-5), the mechanic can take a sample of coolant vapor from the radiator filler neck. The sample passes through a special blue fluid in the analyzer. If exhaust gas is present in the vapor, the fluid turns yellow. The engine then must be disassembled to find and fix the leak.

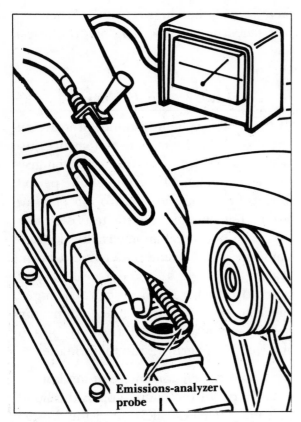

Figure 10–5 An exhaust-gas emissions analyzer

Flushing the Cooling System

One of the most important maintenance routines you must do to prevent overheating involves flushing the cooling system to rid it of corrosion. Corrosion can cause a blockage, and if coolant can't flow freely, it won't cool the engine effectively. Therefore, the cooling system should be flushed every two years. If you don't want to do the job yourself, have a professional mechanic do it.

Drain old coolant and use a flushing T, which is also called a coolant flushing adapter, attached to a garden hose. Follow instructions that accompany the T. Make sure the flow of water through the cooling system also flushes the heater core by turning the heater on and setting the temperature control to the full-heat position. Allow the entire system to flush for about 15 minutes; then refill the cooling system with fresh coolant. Purge the air from the system using the procedure given in the manufacturer's repair manual.

<u>Note</u>: Consult the owner's manual or repair manual for the recommended proportions of ethylene glycol (antifreeze) to water necessary to protect your engine from temperatures in your area. In most parts of the United States, a 50:50 ratio is adequate.

Unfortunately, flushing rarely solves serious cooling system blockage caused by long-term neglect. If the water that comes out of your radiator looks rusty after flushing, use a chemical cleaner to try to get the system clean. (Follow the instructions on the container.) If rust doesn't clear up, the radiator is probably clogged; have the cooling system cleaned professionally by a radiator shop.

11

The Suspension System

TROUBLESHOOTING BRIEF

The suspension system receives a great deal of punishment. Shock absorbers, springs, and motor mounts are constantly being battered by bumps, potholes, and other road-bed imperfections. Tires and wheels are also considered parts of the suspension system, and even normal driving subjects them to wear and tear. Almost certainly, sooner or later, damage to one or more suspension parts will alter how your car handles.

The suspension system telegraphs the presence of problems to you through vibrations felt in the car seat, floor, or steering wheel. Vibration may also be visible; the hood may shake or the steering wheel may oscillate.

This chapter discusses how to determine whether vibration is signaling damage to the suspension system and, if so, how to pinpoint the affected component. The troubleshooting material is divided into two sections: for rear-wheel-drive cars and for front-wheel-drive cars.

Note: Steering system components are mentioned throughout the chapter. Suspension and steering, although distinct systems, are inseparable. What affects one usually affects the other. Therefore, the vibration may not be originating from a worn suspension system part (although that's usually the case), but from a damaged steering system component.

PROJECT DATA

Special tools and materials. Manufacturer's repair manual, safety stands, tachometer. **Job difficulty and time.** Degree of difficulty is relative to the mechanic's experience; all times are approximate.

- Troubleshooting smooth-road shake: Easy, 15 minutes.
- Test driving to check soundness of rear-wheel-drive car suspension system: Easy, 30 minutes.
- Stationary testing of rear-wheel-drive car suspension system components: Easy to difficult, 45–60 minutes.
- Testing shock absorbers: Easy to difficult, 30–90 minutes.
- Test driving to check soundness of front-wheel-drive car suspension system: Easy, 15 minutes.
- Stationary testing of front-wheel-drive car suspension system components: Difficult, 60 minutes.

Safety precautions. Whenever possible, make under-the-car inspections without raising the vehicle. Make certain, however, that you engage the parking brake and put an automatic transmission in Park and a manual transmission in gear.

- Exercise great care if you must raise the vehicle. You could be seriously injured or killed if the car falls down. Always use safety stands, or, if the inspection does not require you to manipulate the wheel, use safety ramps. Never support a car with a jack.
- Raise a car on firm, level ground. Before you raise the front end of a car, engage the parking brake, place the car in Park (automatic transmission) or in gear (manual transmission), and put chocks behind the rear wheels. When you raise the rear end of a car, be aware that the parking brake engages the rear wheels. Therefore, to prevent the car from rolling, *always* place chocks in front of the front wheels. Whenever possible use safety ramps instead of safety stands. As an added precaution, put a front-wheel-drive car in Park or in gear.

Vibration in a Rear-Wheel-Drive Car

Smooth-road shake (SRS) is a characteristic vibration from a rear-wheel-drive car that is important to recognize. The vibration is apparent while driving on a smooth road. It also occurs on a rough road, but on a rough road you expect some form of vibration and might overlook the phenomenon.

Smooth-road shake occurs only at highway cruising speeds. Technically, it is a vibration associated with a frequency equivalent to one tire revolution; in other words, a vibration consisting of 12 cycles per second when a car is moving at 55 mph. (SRS is *not* a low-speed shimmy. If what you are feeling is a low-speed shimmy, one or more of the tires may have a broken reinforcing belt. Examine the tires for metal fibers protruding through the tread.)

Car components have production tolerances that manufacturers try to stay within. Sometimes, however, small problems compound into larger ones. For example, tires are not perfectly round or uniform; resiliency varies around their circumferences. Wheel dimensions also vary, and many factors can cause a wheel to rotate imperfectly (see Figure 11-1). In addition, everyday driving can easily throw wheels out of balance and alignment. SRS results when two or more variations occur simultaneously.

Road Test for SRS   To find out if a vi-

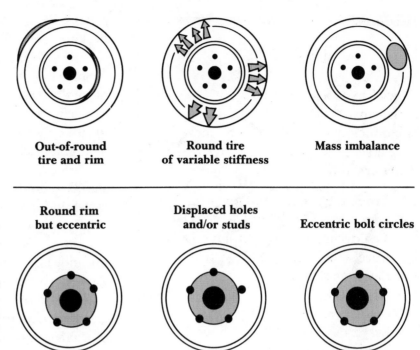

Out-of-round tire and rim   **Round tire of variable stiffness**   **Mass imbalance**

Round rim but eccentric   **Displaced holes and/or studs**   **Eccentric bolt circles**

Figure 11–1 Common causes of smooth-road shake

Illustrated here are six wheel and tire malfunctions to have checked if your car is experiencing smooth-road shake.

bration coming from your rear-wheel-drive car is smooth-road shake, follow these steps:

1. Find a smooth road with no bumps, chuck holes, scalloped surfaces, or grooved sections.

<u>Caution:</u> Do the drive-train vibration test when no other vehicles are in sight. Although the test takes a few seconds, keep a watch out for any vehicle approaching from the rear. Shift back into gear at once and accelerate to normal speed if you spot a car.

2. Drive the car to determine if the shake is speed-sensitive. Start off slowly and gradually build up speed. If present, SRS will develop as you approach a speed of 50 to 60 mph and fade as you go above this speed.

3. Check to see if the vibration is coming from the drive train: the transmission, drive shaft, differential, or rear axles. Put the transmission in Neutral as the car cruises at the speed at which you feel vibration.

If a drive-train component is causing vibration, you will not feel it as the car coasts. A vibration from the drive train should be checked by a mechanic. If the vibration continues, the drive train is not at fault. The vibration stems from a worn part of the suspension or steering system. Before taking the car to a mechanic, you may want to try to pinpoint the fault yourself.

The Suspension and Steering Systems

Worn parts of the suspension and steering systems are a major cause of vehicle instability, as well as vibration. If you disregard symptoms and allow parts to wear excessively, your safety can be jeopardized. Therefore, whether you choose to examine the suspension and steering systems yourself or have a mechanic do it, make sure all components are checked.

Road Test Before undertaking shop procedures, continue your road test. You may be able to get a line on which part of the suspension or steering system is causing the problem.

1. Make sure the road on which you're doing the test is level and not crowned. A

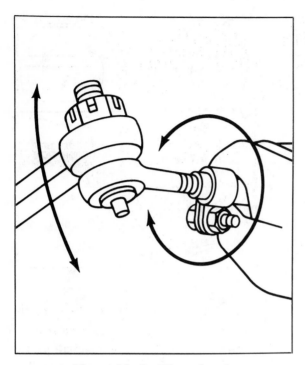

Figure 11–2 Tie-rod ends

crowned road will cause the car to steer toward the shoulder—giving a false indication of what's wrong. A pull or drift to one side on a level road usually suggests faulty wheel alignment. Hold the steering wheel lightly, and drive with the car aimed down the center of the lane. A sound suspension and steering system will keep the car in the center. Assuming that tires are properly inflated, any pull to one side is cause for concern.

2. Make some turns. You shouldn't have to wrestle the steering wheel back to center; it should return practically by itself. If you have to turn the wheel excessively, it suggests that the steering gear is binding or the steering-axis inclination angle is incorrect and has to be readjusted on a wheel alignment machine.

3. Drive over railroad tracks to check the condition of shock absorbers. Of all the suspension system components, shocks are the most susceptible to wear and damage. If the car bounces excessively, suspect worn

shocks. Bad shocks alter riding comfort, braking, and handling.

Some of the inspections that follow require that you crawl under the car; do those inspections with the car wheels on the ground. A flashlight should prove useful. You must jack up the car to perform a few of the tests, in which case you *must* use safety stands to do those procedures safely. Never crawl under a car when it's supported by a jack; you could be crushed if the jack fails.

Caution: Raise a car only on firm, level ground. Place an automatic transmission in Park or a manual transmission in gear. Then, set the parking brake and place chocks behind the rear wheels. Lift the front of the car high enough with a scissors jack to place stands under the left and right control arms. Slowly lower the car until it is supported by the safety stands. If the stands shift, raise the car and reposition the stands.

Tie-rod Ends   With the car wheels on the ground, check that the parking brake is on and that the car is in Park or in gear. Slide under the car and push up and down on the tie rods (see Figure 11-2). Watch the rod sockets for any movement. Then, roll the tie rod while observing the socket movement. If the rod rolls easily, the socket needs replacement. Double-check the diagnosis by having an assistant move the steering wheel while you check for excessive play at the tie rod.

Wheel Bearings   Raise the car as described in the "Caution" above, and grasp the front tire at the top and bottom (see Figure 11-3). Rock a front wheel. It should be firm, with nearly no movement between wheel and spindle. Test both front wheels. Noticeable movement usually indicates loose wheel bearings; they should be cleaned, repacked with grease, and adjusted.

Side Play   With the wheels straight, grasp the tire at the front and rear (see

Figure 11–3 Testing the wheel bearings

Figure 11-4). Check tires for side play. If side play is present, bushings, adjustment clamps, and ball joints should be checked for wear. A loose steering gear, idler arm, or pitman arm may also be the problem. A mechanic may be able to make adjustments to take up any steering looseness.

Ball Joints Identify the weight-carrying

Figure 11–4 Testing for side play

ball joint. It's always mounted in the control arm attached to the spring or torsion bar. The other ball joint is the friction ball joint, which steadies the other end of the spindle. To check for wear, use a floor jack to take the weight off the load-carrying joint. Use a pry bar between the bottom of the tire and the ground to check for excessive radial play (see Figure 11-5). Some ball joints have wear indicators; your car's repair manual will show you the details.

Drag With floor jack in the same position used to check the weight-carrying ball joint, rotate the wheels (see Figure 11-6). Listen for growling from the wheel bearings. Next feel for signs of dragging from either worn wheel bearings or a brake caliper frozen in the "brakes-on" position. A steering pull that feels like an alignment problem is often actually caused by one of these other problems.

Steering Systems Lower the car so that the wheels rest on the ground. Identify your steering system (see Figure 11-7). Parallelogram steering combines tie rods, rod ends, idler and pitman arms, and center link connected to a steering gear. Rack-and-pinion steering is the system of choice in modern cars. To maintain proper wheel alignment

Figure 11–5   Testing the weight-bearing ball joints

With a torsion-bar system, the spring action comes from a steel bar that is under torsional load. One end of the bar is usually splined to the control arm, the other end is firmly attached to the vehicle's frame. As the road irregularities act on the arm, the bar twists and untwists, absorbing energy before it's transmitted to the body. Look for damage to the bar.

An A-arm system has four critical wear points: the upper and lower control-arm bushings and the upper and lower ball joints. A worn control-arm bushing allows the arm to move, and may sometimes manifest itself as a dull knock when you brake or accelerate. To check ball joints, first determine whether the coil spring is seated on the upper or lower control arm. If the spring is seated .on the upper arm, jack the car under the body or frame to check the ball joint for looseness. If the spring is seated on the lower arm, jack the car under the arm to unload the joints for inspection. Follow the safety precautions given earlier.

and accurate steering response, both types must be free of wear.

Tire Tread   Look for tire-wear patterns that are clues to front-end problems. For example, toe-in is the difference in distance between the front and rear edges of the two front tires as measured at hub height (see Figure 11-8). Feather-edge wear occurs when toe-in is incorrectly set, because driving drags the tire sideways.

If the inner third of the tire is worn smooth and the outer third still has plenty of tread, it's a sign of camber misadjustment (Figure 11-8). Camber is the inward or outward tilt of the wheel. Negative camber results in excessive inner-tire wear.

Shock Systems   Identify the type of front-end suspension system your rear-wheel-drive car has, either torsion bar (see Figure 11-9) or A-arm (see Figure 11-10). <u>Caution</u>: Use safety stands or ramps to make the following inspections: follow the precautions given earlier.

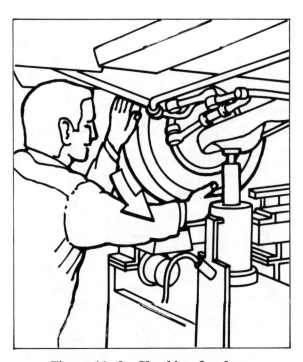

Figure 11–6   Checking for drag

Figure 11–7 Steering systems

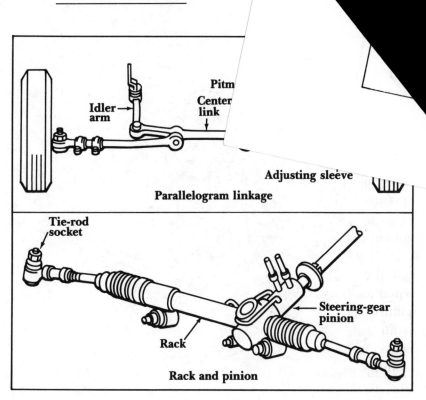

Idler arm

Pitm

Center link

Adjusting sleeve

Parallelogram linkage

Tie-rod socket

Steering-gear pinion

Rack

Rack and pinion

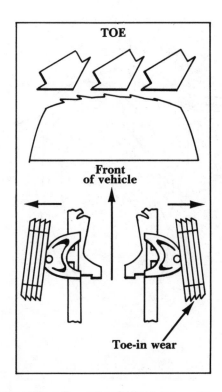

TOE

Front of vehicle

Toe-in wear

CAMBER

Positive camber

Figure 11–8 Tire-tread wear

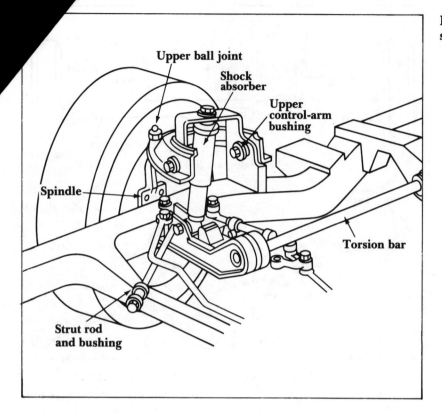

Upper ball joint

Shock
absorber

Upper
control-arm
bushing

Spindle

Torsion bar

Strut rod
and bushing

**Figure 11–9   Torsion-bar
suspension system**

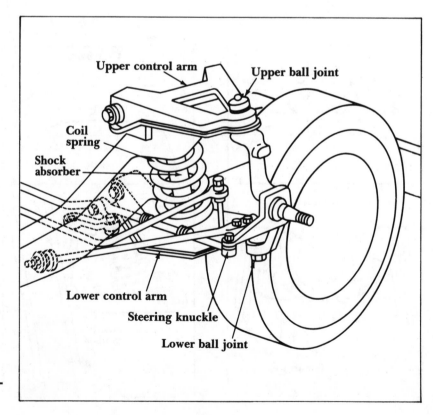

Upper control arm

Upper ball joint

Coil
spring

Shock
absorber

Lower control arm

Steering knuckle

Lower ball joint

**Figure 11–10   A-arm sus-
pension system**

Shock Absorbers

To pin vibration and ride instability definitely on bad shock absorbers, examine the four of them by raising the car and looking at mounting bushings and connections at both ends of each shock. Caution: Raise one end of the car at a time, following the guidelines given in "Safety Precautions" and on page 92. Since the following inspections do not require that you manipulate the wheel, use safety ramps to raise the rear end of the car, particularly if the car has front-wheel drive. Bolts should be tight. Rubber bushings should not be broken, loose, chipped, or missing. If there is damage, replace the shocks.

Check for fluid leaking from where the shaft of each shock goes into the shock body. If sheathing covers the shaft, but the body of the shock is damp, it is probably leaking. As a shock loses fluid, its ability to offset the oscillations transmitted by springs is lost: replace the shocks.

If all four shock absorbers have been in use for many miles, and one goes bad, all four should be replaced. If the others aren't already defective, they soon will be. What defines high mileage for shocks varies, but 25,000 miles is an average life span for original-equipment shocks.

If your shock absorbers have low mileage on them, and you find one bad shock, you need not replace all four. For example, if the shocks have been in use 5,000 miles and one goes bad, you need only replace that one and its mate: both front shocks if one is bad, both rear shocks if one is bad.

If the shocks are not leaking, lower the car and do the bounce test. With the car parked on a level surface, stand at a corner of the vehicle and push down and release the car. Perform the test at all four corners. If a corner bounces more than one and one half times, the action of the shock in that corner has deteriorated: replace the shocks as necessary.

If you have any doubt about the condition of shock absorbers after inspecting them and performing the bounce test, there is one sure check. Disconnect the bottom of each shock absorber, and pull on the shock until it is fully extended. Then, with short up-and-down strokes, gradually move the bottom of the shock upward until it is fully compressed. If there's any place along the way where there is no resistance, the shock is in bad condition.

Note: Sometimes the arrangement of shock absorber mounts does not permit you to perform the compression test with the top part of shocks still attached to the vehicle. In that case, remove shocks from the car one at a time. Tighten one end in a bench vise and do the compression test that way.

Replacement Shock Absorbers Although the manufacturer's repair manual for your car will have instructions for replacing the shock absorbers, you may want to have a professional mechanic do the job, since the job can be time consuming.

Shocks that are the same as the original-equipment shocks are, of course, suitable replacements. Heavy-duty shocks, on the other hand, will give a firmer ride and last longer. If your car is old and the suspension has started to sag a little, consider gas or air shocks, or shocks with helper springs. Each upgrade, of course, costs you more.

If your car sags severely—if one corner of the car is several inches lower than the others—even new heavy-duty shocks may not solve the problem. You often have to replace the bad spring, along with its companion spring for the wheel on the other side. Just as with shocks, springs should be replaced in pairs.

If you frequently carry heavy loads in your car, pickup truck, or van and you find that the rear of the vehicle sags as a result, another type of shock, the self-leveler, works well for heavy loads. When a load lowers suspension height, a pair of self-leveler shocks converts the vehicle's bouncing motion into a lifting force capable of raising up to 1,000 pounds. The shocks also work independently and automatically compensate if one side sags lower than the other.

Wheel-Balancing Methods

If you have not yet been able to determine the cause of smooth-road shake or vibration, a mechanic will have to test and calibrate the suspension with instruments. Wheel balancing is one such corrective measure. There are three different methods: on-the-car and off-the-car spin balancing (both are called dynamic balancing) and bubble balancing (or static balancing).

As their names imply, the first two methods balance tire and wheel assemblies while they are in motion. On-the-car spin balancers do the most accurate job, because the instruments balance the entire rotating unit—wheel, tire, hub, axle, and brake drum or rotor—not just the wheel and tire. But once balanced, a wheel should not be moved from that position. Since a wheel and the tire it supports are balanced along with the other parts of the wheel assembly, moving the unit throws balance off.

Off-the-car spin balancing allows you to mount a balanced wheel-and-tire assembly anywhere on the car, without upsetting balance. But the method does not compensate for imbalance in other rotating members.

Bubble-balancing is a stationary procedure. The mechanic mounts each tire and wheel assembly on a leveling apparatus, and attaches weights to the off-balance side of the wheel. A bubble centers itself in a sight glass when the assembly is in balance. Bubble-balancing may eliminate an imbalance

that makes a tire hop, but not an imbalance that makes it wobble.

Other Mechanic's Tasks In addition to balancing, the mechanic should check for worn or damaged suspension- and steering-system components, tire damage, brake-drum and rotor damage, drive-shaft cleanliness, wheel-bearing adjustment, and lug-nut torque.

If none of the above eliminates vibration, the mechanic should check wheels and tires for excessive runout, which is a deviation from concentricity (roundness), plane of rotation (wobble), or both. Runout in excess of repair-manual specification may be caused by a bent wheel. If so, replace the wheel. An out-of-round tire can also cause runout. Grinding tire tread to true may correct the condition, but if it doesn't, you should replace the tire.

Finally, the mechanic should align wheels using four-wheel alignment equipment, which is also called total wheel alignment.

Vibration in a Front-Wheel-Drive Car

Front-wheel drive (FWD) is characteristic of most 1982 and newer cars. A car with front-wheel drive has the engine, transmission, and differential coupled together in front to use the front wheels as the driving wheels. The drive train (transmission and differential) in a car with front-wheel drive is frequently referred to as the transaxle (see Figure 11-11).

If your front-wheel-drive car develops a shimmy, determine whether you are feeling a vibration or an oscillation. A steering wheel that shakes from side to side indicates oscillation. If the steering wheel shakes up and down when the car is at idle or is rolling, the problem is vibration.

Oscillation is most often caused by tire-

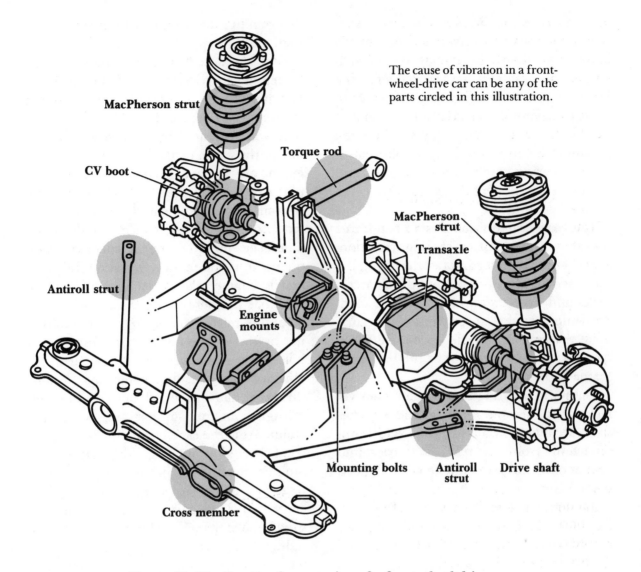

MacPherson strut

The cause of vibration in a front-wheel-drive car can be any of the parts circled in this illustration.

CV boot

Torque rod

MacPherson strut

Transaxle

Antiroll strut

Engine mounts

Mounting bolts

Antiroll strut

Drive shaft

Cross member

Figure 11–11   Front-end suspension of a front-wheel-drive car

wheel imbalance, wheel damage, excessive lateral runout, or brake-rotor runout. Lateral runout refers to wear on the outer edges of a tire. It can cause the tire and wheel to wobble. As measured with a tread gauge at the shoulder (outer edge) of the tire, lateral runout should not exceed the specification in the repair manual (about two millimeters). If it does, replace the tire.

Brake-rotor runout results in oscillation felt only when brakes are applied. A mechanic should measure the surface of rotors for trueness. A warped rotor, or one that is otherwise not true to the manufacturer's specifications, should be shaved on a machine lathe—or replaced if machining would exceed the minimum thickness standard given in the repair manual.

If you feel a vibration from your front-wheel-drive car at idle, check the engine's idling speed. If it's even slightly below specification, the engine can roll against its supports and cause vibration.

If the steering wheel shakes up and down

while the car is moving, verify that accessory mounting bolts and drive belts are not too loose, too tight, or damaged. Tighten mounting bolts to the limits specified by the manufacturer in the repair manual. Also, carefully examine all accessory mounting brackets for cracks. Accessories include the air-conditioning compressor, alternator, power-steering pump, starter motor, and any other component that's attached to the engine by a bracket.

Tachometer and Road Tests If none of the above problems is causing vibration, connect a tachometer and test the car on the road (see Figure 11–12). Shut off all accessories and close the windows. On the road, determine at what speed vibration occurs. Take the car beyond this speed, shift into Neutral, and take your foot off the accelerator pedal.

Caution: Do this test only when other vehicles aren't in sight. Although the test takes a few seconds, stay alert for any vehicle approaching from the rear. Shift back into gear at once and accelerate to normal speed if you spot an approaching car.

As the car coasts down, notice if you still feel vibration. If you do, the trouble is probably caused by excessive radial runout. Radial runout refers to the difference between high and low spots on the tire's tread. Balancing the wheel and tire assembly can sometimes correct vibration from this fault. If balancing doesn't solve the problem, the tire should be replaced.

If you feel no vibration while coasting down, the cause of the problem lies in the engine or transaxle. To find out which component is at fault, stop the car and put the transmission in Neutral. Speed up the engine until the tachometer reads the revolutions per minute (rpm) at which vibration occurred. If you feel any vibration the problem is engine-related. If not, you have a transaxle problem.

Engine-related problems are often caused not by the engine but by components that hold the engine to the frame or control engine motion: the engine mounts (usually three) and the torque rod (or anti-roll strut).

Engine mounts support and isolate the engine from the car's frame; the torque rod controls engine pitching. Although engine mounts and the engine torque rod might wear and allow the engine to vibrate, the culprits causing engine-related vibration are usually bolts that are either too loose or too tight.

Figure 11–12 A test tachometer wired to run a road test

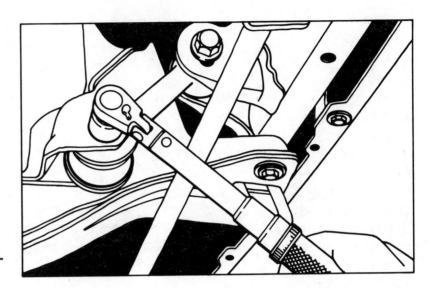

Figure 11–13 Using a torque wrench to tighten torque-rod bolts to specification

Start by refastening the engine-mount bolts. Loosen each bolt and then use a torque wrench to tighten it to the specifications in the repair manual. Resecure not only the engine-mount bolts, but also the bolts that hold the engine mounts to the cross-member.

Retest the car to see whether you've solved the problem. If not, turn your attention to the torque rod, which is a long rod with large rubber bushings at each end. One end is attached to the cross-member, the other to the car body. As the engine tries to roll fore and aft, the torque rod restrains it while rubber bushings absorb vibration. Check to see whether bushings are in good shape; then, loosen the torque-rod bolts and retighten them to the specification in the shop manual (see Figure 11–13). Retest the car.

If you still feel vibration, check the cross-member support bolts. See that they are all installed—someone on the production line may have failed to insert one. Loosen each and retighten it to specification.

MacPherson Struts

Cars with front-wheel drive don't have conventional shock absorbers in the front (and may not in the rear). Instead, they have a MacPherson strut at each front wheel. If you can't spot a conventional shock absorber at each rear wheel, you'll know there's a MacPherson strut there as well.

The MacPherson strut has advantages and drawbacks. On the plus side, it is compact and lightweight. The upper control arm is eliminated, which makes it ideal for small cars. On the minus side, the absorbing unit is a cartridge that's inside the strut. This makes replacement more expensive.

There are two styles of MacPherson struts: those with a spring attached to the strut (see Figure 11–14) and those with a separate spring. Specific removal and reinstallation procedures of MacPherson units vary for different cars. A repair manual is needed.

You cannot replace the strut cartridge, which is the equivalent of a shock absorber, in a strut with an attached spring without using a special tool that compresses the strut spring before the old cartridge can be removed from inside the strut. This tool costs from $150 to $200 and *must* be used to prevent the spring from flying off and possibly causing serious injury. Replacing struts with attached springs and aligning the wheels is

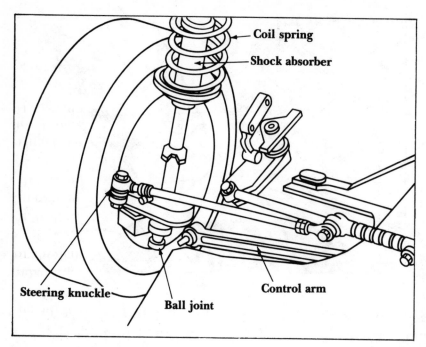

Coil spring

Shock absorber

Steering knuckle

Ball joint

Control arm

Figure 11–14 MacPherson strut with strut cartridge

Servicing of spring-encased struts should not be attempted without a spring-compressor tool.

best left to a mechanic. Cars with Mac-Pherson struts must have their front wheels aligned after the struts have been worked on.

To replace a MacPherson strut with a separate coil spring yourself, you need to raise the car and support it with a jack stand under the lower control arm. Caution: Follow the guidelines given under "Safety Precautions" on page 90. Remove the wheel and upper and lower mounting bolts, then lift the strut out. You must then remove the cartridge. If the cartridge is not set up to be removed, the entire assembly has to be replaced. The repair manual explains the procedure. If special tools are needed to remove a cartridge and you can't borrow them, have a mechanic do the job for you. In any case, you must have the wheels aligned by a professional after the Mac-Pherson struts are replaced.

12

Brakes

TROUBLESHOOTING BRIEF

Most cars have disc brakes up front and drum brakes in the rear. A few performance and luxury models have disc brakes front and rear. Most cars built before 1979 have drum brakes front and rear. This chapter describes how to recognize a brake system malfunction and what to do about it.

It is recommended that only professional mechanics do brake jobs. Troubleshooting and replacing disc-brake pads and drum-brake linings are tasks that some do-it-yourself mechanics may want to try, but they should do so only if they have the manufacturer's repair manual and the necessary tools.

PROJECT DATA

Special tools and materials. Manufacturer's repair manual, safety stands, hand-held vacuum pump with fluid reservoir, respirator with a filter approved for asbestos fibers, star-wheel adjuster.

Possible replacement parts. Brake pads or linings, master cylinder, hydraulic brake lines, wheel cylinders. (See "Cautionary Notes" on p. 106.)

Job difficulty and time. Degree of difficulty is relative to the mechanic's experience; all times are approximate.

- Road testing to judge the condition of a brake system: Easy, 15 minutes.
- Part-by-part examination of a brake system: Difficult, 60 minutes.

Safety precautions. Brakes are essential safety devices; diminished brake performance or brake failure can lead to a serious or even fatal accident. If you make a repair poorly or improperly, you put yourself and others at great risk. Therefore, do not undertake any brake work unless you have the experience, tools, and information needed to do the job correctly.

- Exercise great care if you must raise the vehicle. You could be seriously injured or killed if the car falls down. Even though you cannot use safety ramps when you troubleshoot the brakes, because the work involves removing tires, always use safety stands. Never support a car with a jack.
- Raise a car on firm, level ground. Before you raise the front end of a car, engage the parking brake, place the car in Park (automatic transmission) or in gear (manual transmission), and put chocks behind the rear wheels. When you raise the rear end of a car, be aware that the parking brake engages the rear wheels. Therefore, to prevent the car from rolling, *always* place chocks in front of the front wheels. As an added precaution, put a front-wheel-drive car in Park or in gear.
- Brake linings for drum brakes may contain asbestos fibers. Inhaling asbestos fibers is hazardous to your health. Always wear a respirator with a filter approved for asbestos fibers when you work on drum brakes.

How a Brake System Works

Foot effort applied to the brake pedal is amplified in most cars by a vacuum-operated power-assist unit (see Figure 12-1). Simultaneously, the master cylinder pressurizes brake fluid in two separate hydraulic circuits. One circuit serves the front brake units, the other serves the rear drum units. This system is frequently referred to as a dual-braking system.

The combination valve contains a metering valve that controls pressure to the front-brake calipers by restricting the flow of brake fluid to them until about 125 pounds per square inch (psi) of pressure has developed. This delays front-brake caliper action just long enough for the slower-reacting rear brakes to engage.

The combination valve also houses a self-centering pressure-differential sensing switch. Should the system develop a brake fluid leak, the switch will block off the hydraulic circuit where the leak has occurred. The switch may also illuminate a dashboard warning light. In the event of a fluid leak, the dual system makes it unlikely that the car will experience total brake failure.

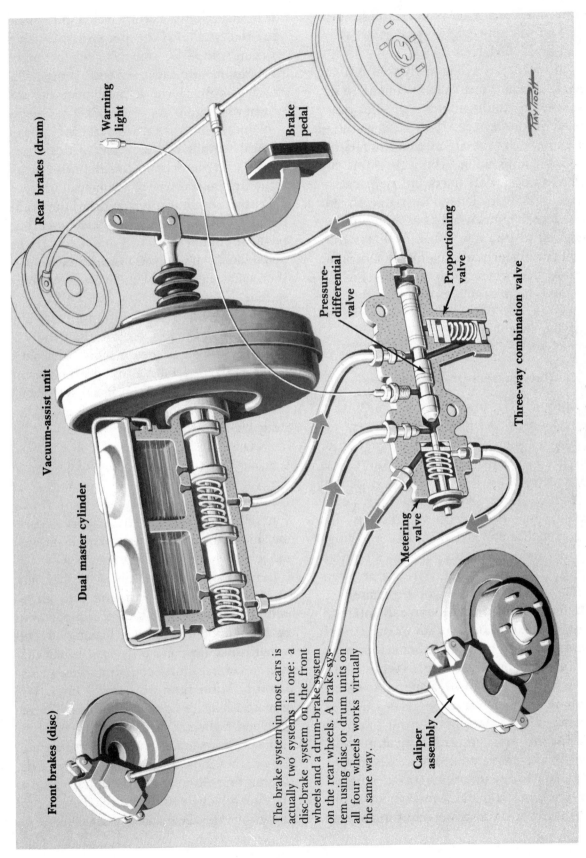

Rear brakes (drum)

Warning light

Brake pedal

Pressure-differential valve

Proportioning valve

Three-way combination valve

Vacuum-assist unit

Dual master cylinder

Metering valve

Front brakes (disc)

Caliper assembly

The brake system in most cars is actually two systems in one: a disc-brake system on the front wheels and a drum-brake system on the rear wheels. A brake system using disc or drum units on all four wheels works virtually the same way.

Figure 12–1 The brake system

Either the front or rear brakes will stop the car. You will notice, however, a lower-than-usual brake pedal.

Many cars have diagonally-split braking systems in which one front brake unit shares the same hydraulic circuit as the rear brake on the opposite side. If there is a loss of fluid in a hydraulic circuit, therefore, either braking combination—the right front and left rear or the left front and right rear—will stop the car, depending on which side fails. The diagonally-split braking system is designed to improve braking stability during hydraulic circuit malfunctions. Some systems have a proportioning valve, which balances the hydraulic pressure to the rear drum brake and helps control rear-wheel skidding.

Recognizing Brake Problems

Symptoms of a brake problem include a lower-than-usual brake pedal that travels excessively far before brakes engage and, conversely, a hard pedal that requires excessive pressure to halt the vehicle. A spongy or fading brake pedal—when the pedal feels soft or falls away under pressure—indicates malfunctions. Grabbing (or pulling) to one side, shuddering, or noises such as grinding sounds, squeaks, or chatter when brakes are applied, all signal problems.

If one of these conditions exists, if you think one exists, but you aren't sure, or if you simply want to test the brake system in your vehicle to make certain it's sound, once every 10,000 miles or so, a simple road test follows.

Road Test Assuming your car is equipped as most are with a vacuum-operated power-assist unit, known as power brakes, park the car and shut off the engine. Pump the brake pedal several times to deplete vacuum in the power-assist unit. Press the brake pedal as far down as it will go and start the engine. If the power-assist unit is working properly, you will feel the pedal drop slightly. Release the pedal. If the pedal doesn't move, have a mechanic test the power-assist unit.

Note: If your car doesn't have power brakes, begin troubleshooting at this point. If your car does have power brakes, continue the procedure.

With the engine running, press the brake pedal lightly and hold it for 60 seconds. The pedal should remain still and firm. If the pedal fades—if it travels towards the floor—there may be a problem in the hydraulic system.

Drive the car at 20 to 30 mph with the steering wheel held loosely in your hands. Apply the brakes. If the car pulls to one side, or the brake pedal fades under pressure, or any of the other conditions listed at the start of the section occurs, your car has a braking system malfunction.

Cautionary Notes

Do not attempt any brake-system repair yourself unless you have the experience, repair manual, and special tools necessary for the job.

Before installing any new brake part, carefully compare it with the old one to make certain you have the correct part. For example, if you replace a leaking or corroded brake line, use only steel brake tubing. Never substitute copper tubing or use a compression fitting on brake lines. Use only specially designed and flared brake lines and fittings.

If you have brake rotors or drums machined, they must be carefully measured before cutting. Removing too much metal is unsafe and can result in overheating and distortion. Measurements must comply with repair manual specifications. For example, it is usually unsafe to remove more than 0.06 inch of metal from a drum surface. <u>Caution:</u> Rotors and drums have a cutting limit stamped into the metal or specified in the repair manual that must not be exceeded: replace the part if too much metal has to be removed.

The error made most often by nonprofessionals who try to overhaul drum brakes is reversing the brake shoes. The professional mechanic who rectifies the problem will find that the primary, or forward, shoe is properly installed on the left rear wheel but incorrectly on the right rear wheel. The right-rear brake setup is a *mirror* image of the opposite side. It is wise to disassemble only one brake at a time so you have an assembled brake to use as a reference. But the two sides do not look exactly alike. A good way to remember how brakes should look on either side is to visualize an arrow at the top of the brake pointing in the direction the drum rotates when the car is moving forward. The primary shoe will always be at the point of the arrow.

Before you reinstall rear brake drums, check that the parking-brake cable is working freely. Cables often rust and seize. Apply penetrating oil to solve this problem. After the drum is on, use a star-wheel adjusting tool to adjust the brake until it begins to drag. Then, back off the adjuster so the wheel rotates freely when the brake is released.

Brake-fluid condition is important. Fluid doesn't last forever since it is prone to absorb moisture when the hydraulic system is opened. Therefore, flush all brake fluid when you replace any hydraulic component. Replace it with a top-quality DOT 3 or 4 fluid, or consider changing to moisture-resistant silicone brake fluid (DOT 5). (DOT stands for U.S. Department of Transpor-

tation. The letters on containers of brake fluid mean that the fluid meets DOT standards.) Use the fluid recommended in the car's owner's manual.

Front Disc Brakes

If when you apply brakes you get a noise, chatter, or shudder, or brakes grab and pull the car to one side, check the front brakes first. Front brakes wear more rapidly and have problems more frequently than rear brakes.

To check front brakes, jack up the car and place it on secure safety stands.

<u>Caution:</u> Raise a car only on firm, level ground. Place an automatic transmission in Park or a manual transmission in gear. Then place chocks behind the rear wheels. Lift the front of the car high enough with a scissors jack to place stands under the left and right control arms. Slowly lower the car until it is supported by the safety stands. If the stands shift, raise the car and reposition the stands.

Take off each wheel and tire assembly in turn, and examine the thickness of disc-brake pads (see Figure 12-2). If pads are thinner than the metal backing plates, they should be replaced.

Reinstall the wheel and tire assembly. Now turn the wheel slowly by hand to determine if it makes a noise or binds at any spot, either of which is reason enough to seek the advice of a service technician.

If the brake pedal is fading under pressure when you apply the brakes, look inside the master cylinder. A low fluid level in one compartment of the cylinder means there's a leak. (The brake system doesn't consume fluid and fluid doesn't evaporate.) Check the hydraulic circuit inch by inch. From the master cylinder, trace each brake line to its respective wheel and look for any signs of fluid. If you find no evidence of a leak, take

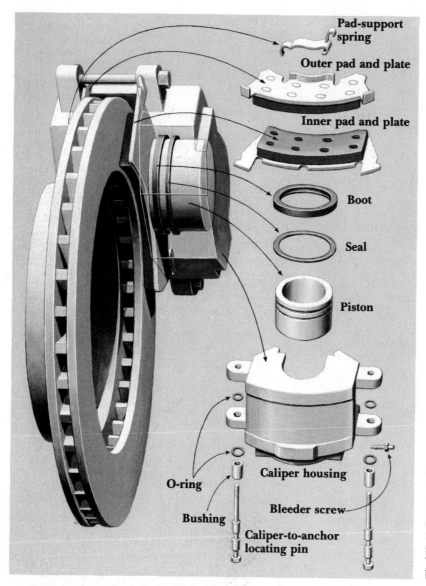

Pad-support spring

Outer pad and plate

Inner pad and plate

Boot

Seal

Piston

Caliper housing

O-ring

Bushing

Bleeder screw

Caliper-to-anchor locating pin

Figure 12–2 Disc brakes

Hydraulic pressure causes the disc-brake caliper piston to move, squeezing the brake pads so they clamp onto the rotor. The resulting friction provides braking force to stop the car.

off each wheel and tire assembly and examine each part of the brake unit for fluid.

Caution: Before removing the wheel and tire assembly, read the section on drum brakes (p. 109) and carefully follow all precautions in it. Drum-brake linings may contain asbestos and the wheel assembly may house asbestos dust; inhaling asbestos dust can harm your health.

If this fails to reveal the leak, remove the master cylinder and check for a leak where the push rod enters the back of the cylinder. There should be no fluid present at *any*

point. If you find fluid, or even if you just suspect a leak, draw the attention of your mechanic to it. Have a professional examine the system.

Air trapped in the hydraulic system causes the brake pedal to feel spongy. Sponginess occurs most frequently after the brake system has been worked on. The system must be purged of air, a process known as bleeding the brakes. You may want to do this yourself. If you don't have an assistant to pump the pedal while you open the bleeder screws at each wheel, you'll need a manual vacuum pump with a fluid reservoir (see Figure 12-3). The repair manual details the specific bleeding procedure for your car.

A squeak from disc brakes is sometimes caused by vibrating brake pads. Check to make sure the antirattle clips that are supposed to prevent vibration are in good condition. Pad-support hardware must also be in place and fit tightly.

Squeaks from disc brakes may signal the need for new brake pads, but if a mechanic confirms that there's no malfunction, content yourself that occasional squeaks are normal. They usually occur when air humidity is high or temperature is low.

With disc brakes, the brake pedal can push back (pulsate) when you press it. This indicates a condition in which a rotor is thicker in one spot than others. When the thicker part of the rotor passes through the caliper, it pushes the piston back into the caliper. You feel this pulsation on your foot. Having rotors machined on a brake lathe usually resolves this condition.

Drum Brakes

Begin any inspection of drum brakes by removing the rear wheel and tire assemblies and brake drums. First, raise the car on a pair of sturdy safety stands.

<u>Caution</u>: An accumulation of gray dust that may contain asbestos can cling to brake shoes and hardware. Inhaling asbestos fibers can be hazardous to your health; you *must* avoid breathing or ingesting this dust. Do *not* disassemble or work on drum brakes without an approved respirator on. A res-

Figure 12–3 Using a manual vacuum pump with a reservoir to bleed brakes

A reservoir holds brake fluid drawn from the nipple of the brake bleeder valve.

pirator with the proper filter can be purchased from an automotive parts dealer.

Raise a car only on firm, level ground. Engage the safety brake and place an automatic transmission in Park or a manual transmission in gear. Place chocks under the front wheel. Raise the car with a jack and place stands under the left and right axle housings. Slowly lower the car onto the safety stands. If the stands shift, raise the car and reposition the stands.

Getting drums off is sometimes difficult. Frequently, a rusty ridge builds up on the drum edge. To remove a stuck drum, first back off the brake adjuster with a star-wheel adjusting tool (see Figure 12-4). This allows the brake shoes to pull back clear of the drum. Apply penetrating oil and tap around the drum with a hammer, especially at the axle flange at the drum's center opening. The drum will eventually free itself. Taking the drum off gives you a clear view of brake shoes and hardware.

Many full-size U.S.-made cars use a duo-servo, anchor-type, self-adjusting drum-brake system (see Figure 12-5). It can be identified by the star-wheel adjuster at the bottom and the fixed anchor pin at the top. When pressure is applied to the brake pedal, the entire duo-servo brake assembly moves against the drum. Force is transferred from the primary brake shoe through the star wheel to the secondary shoe, a process known as servo action. The primary shoe is always closer to the front of the car, and may have a shorter lining. The secondary shoe provides 70 percent of the stopping force. Self-adjuster linkages may use levers or cables. Either way, the movement of the brake shoe turns the star wheel enough to spread the shoes outward toward the drum.

Many small cars, both U.S.-made and imported, use non-servo drum brakes (Figure 12-5). Instead of a star wheel, they use an adjuster assembly. The forward shoe, which is often the longer one, does most of the work.

Lining and Cylinders First, check the thickness of the friction material on the brake shoes. There should be at least $1/32$ inch of material above the rivet heads of riveted linings. If linings are bonded to the

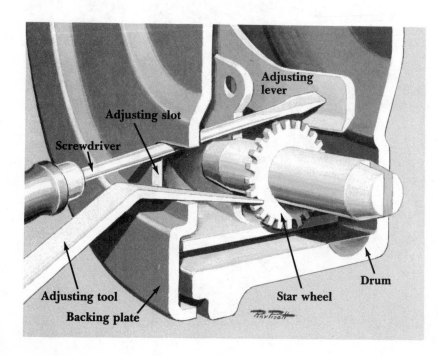

Adjusting lever
Adjusting slot
Screwdriver
Drum
Adjusting tool
Backing plate
Star wheel

Figure 12–4 Using an adjusting tool and screwdriver to back off a star-wheel adjuster

110

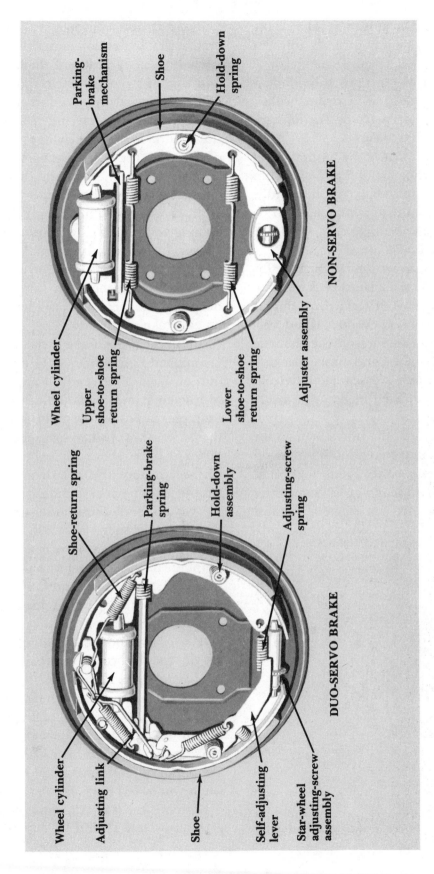

Figure 12–5   Drum brakes

shoes, they should be at least as thick as the shoes. Measure the lining at its thinnest point.

Note: Lining is the term used to identify friction material used with drum brakes. Pad is the name given to the friction material used with disc brakes.

Do not ignore worn brake linings. Rivet heads or brake-shoe metal that makes contact with the drum damages it rapidly. Grooved or scored drums may have to be discarded for new drums or, at the least, resurfaced on a brake lathe.

Continue your inspection by checking for leaking wheel cylinders. Draw back the rubber end covers to see if fluid drips out. It shouldn't; install a new cylinder if it does.

Look for grease leaking from the rear axle onto the brake shoes and brake backing plate. If the rear-axle grease retainer is leaking, it must be replaced before you install new brake linings.

Inspect the back of the brake plate to see that the steel tubing going into it is in good condition. Check all hydraulic tubing and hoses going to both rear wheels. Sometimes rust or abrasion, from a rubbing exhaust pipe, for example, can damage brake tubing.

Figure 12–6 A right-side star-wheel adjuster

Brake Drums Inspect brake drums for cracks. Cracks develop most often at the bolt circle or at the outside of the brake flange and usually become visible only after machining. Discard a cracked drum.

Sometimes the extreme heat generated during braking causes changes in the metal of the drum itself. The heat actually creates spots of steel in the cast-iron drum surface. These hard spots can cause rapid lining wear, chatter, or a "hard" brake pedal. Machining will not usually remove these hard spots. They have to be ground using a special cutter with a grinding-wheel head. In extreme cases, when the hard spots run deep into the metal, you will have to install a new brake drum.

A pulsing of the brake pedal when brakes are applied signals that a rear drum may be out of round (warped). Frequent brake overheating, on long mountain descents, for example, can cause warping. So can setting the parking brake when a drum is extremely hot. The brake shoes applied to the drum's surface prevent the hot drum from contracting to its normal round shape as it cools.

Over a period of time brake drums—particularly wide ones—may also become bell-mouthed; the drum distorts and the shoes cannot make full contact with the drum surface. A bell-mouthed drum can cause brake fade, weak braking, and premature wear on one side of the lining.

If out-of-round or bell-mouthed drums are not too distorted, they may be salvaged by having a brake-repair shop machine them on a brake-drum lathe.

The same heating and cooling cycles that can distort a brake drum also act on the brake return springs. Lively return springs are important, so have new ones installed when you have linings replaced.

Examine the self-adjusting mechanisms carefully. They should be rust-free. Work them by hand to be sure they move smoothly and easily. Have a mechanism that works poorly repaired or replaced.

A low brake pedal on a vehicle with self-adjusting drum brakes can be caused by a star-wheel adjuster with worn or missing teeth. If you find a damaged adjuster, remind your mechanic to install a left adjuster for the driver side and a right adjuster for the passenger side. They're stamped with an L or R (see Figure 12-6).

13

Air-Conditioning and Heating Systems

TROUBLESHOOTING BRIEF

Your car's air conditioner and heater usually work efficiently, but they are subject to some ills. Finding the cause will be easier if you know how these systems operate and follow the troubleshooting routine outlined in this chapter.

Although the air conditioner and heater use common ducts to deliver cool or warm air to the interior of the car, they are two separate systems.

PROJECT DATA

Special tools and materials. Manufacturer's shop manual, thermometer, 12-volt test lamp.

Job difficulty and time. Degree of difficulty is relative to the mechanic's experience; all times are approximate.

- Checking the air conditioner: Easy, 30 minutes.
- Checking the heater: Easy to moderately difficult, 30–45 minutes.

Safety precautions. Wear safety goggles and work gloves when working around air-conditioner hoses and components. An accidental release of refrigerant could freeze your skin or eyes, causing tissue damage.

- Beware of pulleys and belts when the engine is running; never wear loose clothing, watches, rings, or other jewelry when working on a car.
- Never smoke or bring any device that could create a spark near the car. Work outdoors and keep a dry-chemical (class B) fire extinguisher nearby.

The Air Conditioner

To cool a car's interior, the air conditioner absorbs heat from the passenger compartment and carries the heat to where it can dissipate into the air (see Figure 13-1). Chemicals called refrigerants make this possible. Refrigerants are liquids with very low boiling points; they belong to a versatile but problematic class of chemicals called chlorofluorocarbons (CFCs) and will damage the atmosphere if released into it (see page 118). Refrigerant compounds formulated for automobile air conditioners generally carry the designation Refrigerant-12 or simply R-12.

Refrigerant absorbs, carries, and disposes of heat. The refrigerant's ability to change rapidly from a liquid to a vapor and back again as the temperature to which it is subjected changes by only a few degrees enables it to perform those tasks well.

Functionally, the air-conditioning process begins at the evaporator, which is in the firewall separating the passenger and engine compartments. The bulk of the evaporator actually lies inside the passenger compartment.

The evaporator consists of an array of thin metal fins that surround tubes through which refrigerant flows at low pressure. Since at atmospheric pressure R-12 refrigerant boils at minus 22 degrees F, this agent is "ice" cold, to say the least. The cold is transferred to the evaporator fins. By nature heat always flows from hotter to colder substances: in this case from the car's interior to the colder surfaces of the evaporator fins to the frigid liquid refrigerant. A fan draws warm air toward the evaporator fins. The faster the fan speed, the greater the amount of air transferred to the evaporator and, hence, to the refrigerant. As it absorbs heat, the boiling point of R-12 refrigerant is exceeded: the agent boils and becomes a heat-laden vapor. The vapor flows to the compressor next.

Practically, the compressor is the heart of the system. It is driven by a belt controlled by an electromagnetic clutch. The clutch turns the compressor on and off, thus regulating the rate at which refrigerant flows through the system. Placing the vapor under high pressure enhances its ability to rid itself of the heat it carries, which is done by the condenser.

The condenser is mounted in front of the car's radiator so air can pass through its thin metal fins as the car travels. As the heat-

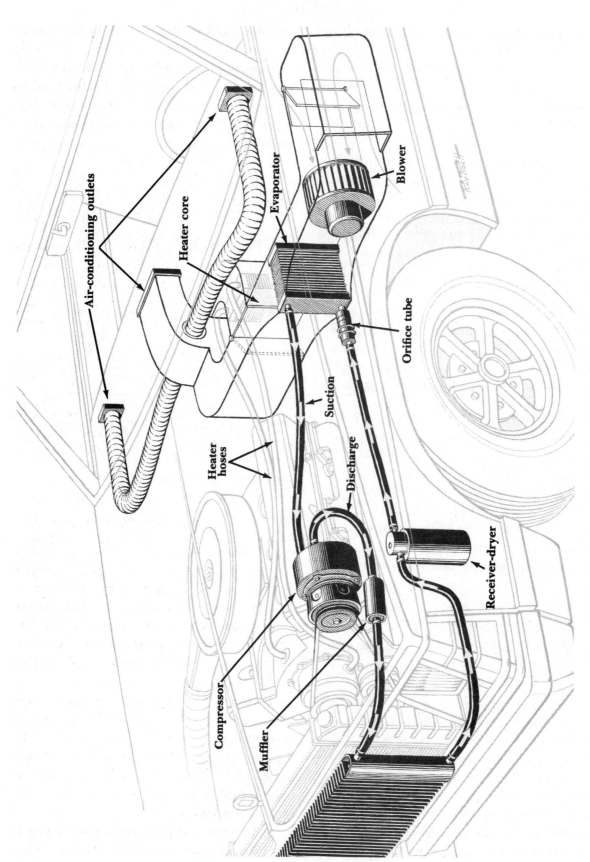

Air-conditioning outlets

Heater core

Evaporator

Blower

Orifice tube

Suction

Discharge

Receiver-dryer

Heater hoses

Compressor

Muffler

Figure 13–1 Typical automobile air-conditioning and heating systems

laden, pressurized vapor flows through the tubes, heat conducted from the refrigerant by the fins is transferred from the fins into the atmosphere. This action lowers the temperature of the refrigerant until it falls below its boiling point, and transforms the agent back into a liquid.

The remaining steps in the refrigerant's circuitous route include passage through a receiver-dryer after it leaves the condenser. The receiver-dryer performs two functions: it filters the refrigerant to remove moisture and holds the refrigerant momentarily before releasing it to the evaporator through an expansion valve, which is a pressure-sensitive metering device.

Not all air conditioners have receiver-dryers. An air conditioner used in many General Motors cars, called the cycling clutch orifice tube (CCOT) system, uses the same major components as other air conditioners, but with two variations. One variation is the use of an accumulator instead of a receiver-dryer. Like a receiver-dryer, the accumulator contains desiccant to filter the refrigerant. However, the accumulator is located at the evaporator outlet, where it filters refrigerant while it's in a low-pressure vaporized state. The receiver-dryer is at the condenser outlet, where it filters the refrigerant while it's in a high-pressure liquid state. The CCOT system also uses an orifice tube, rather than a valve, to depressurize refrigerant fluid before it enters the evaporator.

Working Safely

Do not work on an air conditioner unless you have a repair manual and the proper equipment, and take all necessary precautions. Refrigerant is dangerous and can cause serious injury. Therefore, you are urged to evaluate your capabilities carefully before you proceed. If you are not sure what to do or how to do it, leave troubleshooting to a professional technician. If you decide, however, to do any of the procedures discussed in this section (except for the simple temperature and drive belt checks), make sure you observe the following safety precautions:

- Wear eye protection, gloves, and heavy clothing. Refrigerant sprayed on the skin or in the eyes could cause tissue to freeze.
- Don't inhale refrigerant. Be sure the work area is adequately ventilated.
- Do not transport containers of refrigerants. High temperatures can easily raise pressure in the container to the point where it will explode.
- Avoid doing any steam cleaning or welding near air-conditioner components. Heat from steam cleaning and welding equipment may result in a buildup of pressure that will cause an air-conditioner line or component to rupture.

Air-Conditioner Performance

Close the car doors and windows, turn on the system, and use your hand to feel for cool air at the discharge louvers. Then insert a thermometer into a louver. After the system has cooled the interior for about five minutes, check the temperature. The thermometer should read between 35 and 45 degrees F.

If interior temperature remains high, shut off the engine, raise the hood, and examine the compressor drive belt. Twist the belt to check its underside. If the belt is cracked or has a glazed surface, replace the belt according to the procedure given in the repair manual.

Put on safety goggles and a pair of gloves and inspect air-conditioner hoses for oily-looking areas. An oily appearance signals that the hose is probably leaking, and should be replaced. Continue your inspection by running your gloved hand carefully along the undersides of hoses, feeling for cuts and swelling. A damaged or swollen hose should be replaced.

To replace a hose, the system must be purged of refrigerant. Do *not* vent refrigerant into the atmosphere. As discussed, R-12 refrigerant is dichlorodifluoromethane, part of the chlorofluorocarbon class of chemicals that are commonly known as fluorocarbons. Fluorocarbons are responsible for the well-documented destruction of ozone in the upper atmosphere, where a layer of ozone protects us from harmful ultraviolet rays from the sun. Lost coolant from automotive air-conditioners accounts for an estimated 16 percent of ozone destruction. Therefore purging should be done only by a repair facility that has equipment that will capture refrigerant so it can be recycled.

Check hose fittings for tightness, but be careful not to overtighten them. Caution: Never tighten or loosen a fitting using one wrench. Air-conditioner fittings are fragile, so use the double-wrench technique. Place one wrench to hold the adjacent fitting as you use a second wrench to tighten the primary fitting.

Next inspect the condenser for debris such as leaves and bugs trapped between the fins. Brush any debris out. Look for signs of an oily substance on the condenser that suggests refrigerant leakage. A leaking condenser should be replaced.

If your system has a receiver-dryer, there is probably a sight-glass either on the receiver-dryer or in the line from its discharge side. Turn on the air conditioner, remove the protective cap, and look into the sight-glass. A system that is in good condition will have a clear sight-glass. If you see bubbles, the amount of refrigerant is less than it should be and the system needs recharging. If the system is not cooling and the sight-glass is clear, the system is void of refrigerant, and needs recharging.

Note: If your car has the CCOT system, it doesn't have a sight-glass. If this system is not cooling properly, further troubleshooting is required to determine whether it has lost its refrigerant from a leak or from a broken compressor.

Recharging an air conditioner demands more than simply pumping refrigerant into it. Any remaining refrigerant and moisture must be evacuated, which requires a manifold gauge set and a vacuum pump. The system then needs to be inspected for leaks. All repairs must be made because refrigerant does not just dissipate: an undercharged or empty system has a leak. Finally, charging requires a manifold gauge set and safety can. In short, recharging a system properly is not a task for a layperson; leave it to a professional. In particular, avoid using do-it-yourself recharging cans to replenish refrigerant; refilling a leaky air-conditioning system only adds more CFCs to the atmosphere.

Additional Checks If you have inspected the system and found nothing wrong, but the air conditioner isn't cooling properly, the following checks are suggested:

1. Turn on the interior fan to make sure it is working. If not, check the fan motor's fuse, and replace the fuse if necessary. If the fuse is sound, or if the motor still doesn't run after you've installed a new fuse, the fan needs a new motor.

2. Check the compressor, which must be running for the system to function. Start the engine, turn on the air conditioner, and look at the drive belt to verify that it is turning the compressor pulley without slipping. The

belt may have to be tightened to the specification in the repair manual.

Also, observe the compressor clutch as it cycles (turns on and off). The clutch, which is in the center of the compressor pulley, should click on and the pulley should rotate until the interior of the car has cooled. Then, the clutch should begin to cycle off and on.

If the compressor pulley doesn't begin to rotate when you turn on the air conditioner, probe the electrical connector at the compresser-clutch coil with a 12-volt test light to determine whether the clutch is receiving current. If the lamp lights, the clutch is damaged and the compressor needs an overhaul. If the lamp doesn't light, there is a failure in the electrical circuit to the compressor. In either case, a professional mechanic will probably have to make the repair.

3. If the belt and the compressor clutch work well, but cooling remains insufficient, some part of the system is probably blocked. The receiver-dryer (or accumulator) is the likely culprit, especially if it has been in use for several summers. The actual time it takes for this unit to clog up usually depends on how much the air conditioner is used.

To determine whether a system has a blockage, a mechanic attaches a manifold gauge set to the high- and low-pressure ports of the system to take pressure readings and compare them to the manufacturer's specifications. Various differences between the readings establish if and where a blockage exists. In addition to the receiver-dryer (or accumulator), a hose, the expansion valve (or orifice tube), the evaporator, or the condenser could be blocked. Since testing involves working with pressurized refrigerant and other special equipment, in addition to a manifold gauge set, put the job in the hands of a qualified technician.

4. Although it has nothing to do with the air-conditioning system, the heater control valve may be affecting comfort. A failed valve can, in effect, turn the heater on. The hot air will, of course, counteract the air-conditioning. To check the valve, clamp the heater intake hose to prevent hot coolant from flowing through a possibly defective heater control valve and into the heater core (see page 84). If this action restores the cooling, it proves that the heater control valve is bad, and has to be replaced.

The Heating System

The heating system includes the windshield defroster. If you get little or no heat or inadequate defrosting, the following suggestions may help you pinpoint the trouble:

1. Warm up the engine, turn on the heater, turn the blower to high, and place a thermometer in the path of the air being discharged from the heater outlet. After a few minutes, the reading at the outlet should be 85 to 95 degrees Fahrenheit. A lower temperature indicates a heating system malfunction.

2. Place your hand at the defroster outlet. There should be a strong, steady stream of warm air. If there isn't, but the temperature at the heater outlet is acceptable, the duct that delivers warm air to the defroster outlet has a restriction. A leaking heating core may be the cause of the problem; coolant can pool in the defroster duct and obstruct the flow of air. The smell of antifreeze and steam coming out of the defroster outlet when the engine is warmed up both indicate a leak. To check for leaks, have the heater core removed and put in a tank of water, and have air blown through it. If a stream of air bubbles appears, it verifies a leak. A new heater core is needed.

For the heater to work properly, the engine must be fully warmed up and hot coolant must be flowing through the heater core. Bear in mind: the heater is part of the engine's cooling system (see chapter 10). It is affected, in particular, by the cooling-system thermostat. A thermostat that sticks in a partially or fully closed position restricts the flow of hot coolant to the heater. If there is a lack of heat, therefore, test the thermostat first (see page 84).

If the thermostat passes inspection, check the two heater hoses. One hose feeds hot coolant from the radiator into the heater core; the other returns the coolant to the radiator.

To determine whether hot coolant is flowing properly through the heater core, warm up the engine. Keep the heater off and *carefully* touch the two heater hoses. Both hoses should feel about the same temperature. If you feel a difference, hoses might be bent (be sure they are straight), hoses may have accidentally been reversed (with the intake hose connected to the heater outlet and the outlet hose connected to the heater inlet), or the heater control valve may be defective.

The heater control valve governs the flow of coolant to the heater core. When the heater is off, the valve routes hot coolant to bypass the heater core. When the heater is on, the valve causes hot coolant to flow into the heater core. Thus, if the heater is off, the hoses are straight and connected properly, and the outlet-side hose is *cooler* to the touch than the inlet side hose, the valve is damaged and should be replaced.

If the procedure described to this point fails to reveal the reason for a lack of heat, suspect a clogged heater core. Hot coolant can't flow through a clogged core. You can sometimes purge the core without removing it from the car by doing the following procedure. <u>Caution</u>: Wait for the engine to get cold. Keep the engine off.

1. Disconnect both heater hoses from the heater, but mark or tag each to show the fitting to which it attaches, so you can reconnect the system correctly.

2. Cut two pieces of scrap heater hose, each about 18 inches long. Attach one to the inlet fitting of the heater core and the other to the outlet fitting.

3. Attach a garden-hose adapter to the open end of the outlet hose.

4. Turn on the heater to open the control valve, but keep the engine off. Then attach a garden hose to the adapter and turn the faucet rapidly on and off to try and loosen the clog and flush it out of the heater core with short bursts of water. Give the outlet side four or five bursts before switching the adapter and garden hose to the inlet side to do the same thing.

5. Move the adapter and garden hose back and forth between the two hoses attached to the heater core until the bottleneck is either broken or you give up.

Another method may work to clear a clog in the heater core. Temporarily reverse the positions of the inlet and outlet heater hoses and operate the car with the heater on for a few days. By reversing the flow of coolant, you may be able to dislodge the clog. In the meantime, you won't be able to heat the car, so this isn't the best method for cold weather.

The Duct System

If you still haven't uncovered the reason for lack of heat, the trouble is probably located inside the duct assembly. Most assemblies have doors that operate by vacuum or electric servomotors. If a vacuum hose or a wire is disconnected, the door will remain closed, preventing heat from entering the car.

Electrical problems that affect heater operation involve either the switching system or blower motor. The blower forces air past the heater core, into the interior of the car. If you switch on the heater and blower, but don't feel a stream of air from the heat duct, move the blower switch to another mode. If the blower operates in any other position, the trouble is restricted to the switching system. If you feel no air stream in any switch position, check the blower fuse. If the fuse is good, the blower motor is burned out and will have to be replaced.

Evaluating Your Car's Condition

TROUBLESHOOTING BRIEF

If your automobile is starting to show signs of age, consider this: your car, like your house, is a major investment. Many homeowners stay put and remodel their homes rather than move. Perhaps you should take a close look at your car and decide whether to recondition the car instead of selling it. You may need to spend only a moderate amount of money to retain reasonably reliable transportation. But don't think of reconditioning, or rebuilding, as a restoration. Restoring a car to showroom condition is too expensive if all you want is dependable transportation. Reconditioning means starting with a car that's in reasonably good shape and replacing or repairing as necessary the engine, transmission, suspension, and other operating parts so they'll function for some years to come.

Nevertheless, be aware that you take a gamble when you recondition a car. For example, you may have a good rebuilding job done on those parts that seem to need work, only to have another part fail a few miles later. You'll have to balance the costs, gains, and risks to decide if rebuilding is a good choice for you.

The following tests and inspections can help you tally up the pros and cons of reconditioning your car. All the major items you should investigate are listed. If an item on the list is in good working condition, check "Good." If it needs repair or replacement, check "Bad" and call repair shops to determine how much it will cost to get the repair made.

The Basics

There are some basic questions you should consider when deciding whether to rebuild. You must come to terms with these considerations before committing yourself to reconditioning a car.

1. How much of the work can you do yourself? Consider carefully how long the job will take you and how much time you can realistically devote to the project.

2. What will you do for transportation while the car is in the shop? Consider both cost and convenience.

3. If the car is totalled in an accident or breaks down completely after an expensive rebuilding job, would you be in a financial bind? If your rebuilt car is totalled, the insurance company pays only the book value on it. In fact, it's usually not worthwhile to carry collision coverage on an older car—if you're comfortable with the risk.

4. How much degradation of the car's appearance are you willing to accept? Will you be satisfied with the car's outdated styling? If business reasons or personal taste make appearance an important factor, reconditioning may not be the right course to take.

Basic Questions   If you decide to consider the reconditioning route, first complete Schedule 1. A "yes" answer to any one of the questions indicates that reconditioning would probably be a poor investment. But if your car passes this first test, follow the procedures detailed in the rest of the schedules.

Schedule 1. "Go" or "No-Go" Questions

1. Is the car more than ten years old?   ____yes ____no
2. Is the car expensive to operate?   ____yes ____no
3. Is the car expensive to work on (for example, an imported car or discontinued model with hard-to-get parts)?   ____yes ____no
4. Is the body badly rusted? Do the rocker panels, lower-door panels, or fenders yield to light pressure? Are any of the frame rails or attachments to suspension parts rusted?   ____yes ____no

Road Test   The road test (see Schedule 2) should be done after considering the "go or no-go" questions. It will help you quickly discover some of your car's more obvious faults.

Schedule 2. Stop-and-Go Road Test

Take the car on about a four-mile drive on a variety of roads. Pay close attention to how well the car starts, stops, accelerates, and idles and note any problems. In particular, do the following:

1. Listen carefully to the engine. Knocking sounds may indicate an internal problem, or an imminent transmission failure. A whining noise usually comes from a malfunctioning pump, such as a power-steering pump, or from a housing that contains gears, such as the differential.

Clicking from the top of the engine probably indicates valve-train problems. Tapping sounds indicate any number of problems; try to determine where the tapping comes from so you can investigate the cause.

2. Look for excessive smoke coming from the exhaust pipe. Burning oil creates blue smoke, which is an indication of worn piston rings or leaking valve-stem seals. Black smoke comes from gasoline and is a sign that the fuel mixture is too rich. White "smoke" is usually vapor. It may indicate that coolant has entered one or more of the combustion chambers as a result of a cracked engine head or block or of a bad gasket.

3. Listen to the transmission shifting. An automatic transmission should shift without racing; a standard transmission should shift without grinding gears, and the clutch shouldn't slip between gears.

4. If you can't determine whether a sound comes from the engine or drive train, stop the car and accelerate the engine while the car is in Neutral. If the noise continues, it is engine related; if it doesn't, it comes from the drive train.

5. Note and investigate anything unusual from the road test.

Inspections and Mechanical Tests

After the road test give the underside of the car a thorough going over (Schedule 3), then check the cooling and lubricating systems (Schedule 4). Use earlier chapters as a reference if you're unsure of the procedures.

Schedule 3. Chassis and Undercarriage

1. Check the shock absorbers. If a corner of the car bounces more than one and one half times when you push down on it, the shock is bad. Replace shocks in pairs. ___good ___bad $_____

2. Check the springs. Look for broken spring leaves, bad shackles, signs of shifting, worn rubber bushings, broken shock supports, uneven droop between sides and uneven curb heights. Replace springs in pairs.
    a. Coil springs ___good ___bad $_____
    b. Leaf springs ___good ___bad $_____

3. Check the steering linkage while an assistant moves the wheel.
    a. The tie rods, center link, idler arm, and pitman arm should have free play. ___good ___bad $_____
    b. If the above (a) seem fine, but there is still free play, the steering gear is probably bad. ___good ___bad $_____

4. Inspect all brake lines and hose fittings. ___good ___bad $_____

5. Check the brakes and wheels.

    a. Brake drums and rotors must have enough metal to be turned.

    __good __bad $_____

    b. Brake shoes or pads must be replaced if worn.

    __good __bad $_____

    c. If the brakes fade, the pedal pressure is inconsistent, or you find that the master cylinder leaks: replace the master cylinder.

    __good __bad $_____

    d. Make certain the wheel bearings are sound and well greased.

    __good __bad $_____

6. Inspect the fuel system lines, gauge connections, wires, line supports, and hose connections.

    __good __bad $_____

7. Check the exhaust system. If it is defective, you can probably hear it. Look for rot and cracks.

    __good __bad $_____

8. Inspect all electrical wiring, especially the battery cables and ignition wiring.

    __good __bad $_____

9. Check the "high mortality" parts, such as the battery, radiator cap, fuel filter, and all belts and hoses.

    __good __bad $_____

10. Check the tires. Be sure they have plenty of tread and undamaged sidewalls.

    __good __bad $_____

    Total $_____

Schedule 4. Cooling and Lubricating Systems

1. Pressurize the radiator and look for leaks on the radiator core, heater core, and from hoses and at all hose connections.

    a. Check hoses. Leaking hoses are relatively inexpensive to replace.

    __good __bad $_____

    b. Check the radiator. A leaking radiator core must be soldered or replaced.

    __good __bad $_____

    c. Test the heater core. Replacing a leaking heater core can be expensive.

    __good __bad $_____

    d. Check the condition of the antifreeze. Oily, foamy, or discolored coolant may signal engine problems; rust suggests a blockage in the cooling system.

    __good __bad $_____

2. Check for engine-oil leaks. Have the engine steam-cleaned and then go over it top to bottom.

    a. A leak may be easy to fix, and involve only tightening a valve cover or oil filter. Replacing a valve cover is usually moderately difficult, and can take up to an hour and a half. A leaking rear-main (crankshaft) seal is difficult and expensive to replace; repair may demand that the engine be removed.

    ____good   ____bad $_____

    b. If the engine oil is milky, coolant has leaked into it. Have the engine checked by a professional mechanic.

    ____good   ____bad $_____

3. Check for transmission and differential fluid leakage.

    a. A leaking pan gasket or speedometer gear seal is relatively easy to replace.

    ____good   ____bad $_____

    b. A leaking input-shaft or output-shaft seal is expensive to replace; the engine often has to be pulled.

    ____good   ____bad $_____

    c. If the transmission oil is discolored or smells bad, the transmission probably needs an overhaul. Have a repair shop inspect the transmission.

    ____good   ____bad $_____

    d. Check the differential case for leaks. Replacing a bad seal is expensive.

    ____good   ____bad $_____

    e. Check for leaks where the axles fit into the differential housing. Leaks indicate a worn axle carrier assembly; a moderately expensive repair.

    ____good   ____bad $_____

                     Total $_____

If after your inspection of the chassis, undercarriage, and cooling and lubricating systems the needed repairs and expense of making them seem manageable, go over the engine, or have a professional do the tests for you.

Evaluating the Engine

Check the engine using Schedule 5. If your engine has been performing well and a check of compression, oil pressure, and vacuum show that they're within specification, the engine is probably sound. But be aware that it's easy to be misled when you're working on an engine—even if you're fairly knowledgeable.

Suppose the engine consumes too much oil, but compression is at specification. Logic dictates that the engine needs new valve seals. But valve seals may be only part of the story. Worn rod bearings may be throwing off more oil than the piston rings can handle, and the excess oil on the cylinder walls could be responsible for a misleading compression gauge reading.

In that case, replacing the seals won't help much. A pressure-gauge reading taken at the oil-sender hole would probably tell you about the worn bearings—but maybe not. A low oil-pressure reading might be caused by nothing more than a stuck relief valve in the pump or a plugged oil-pump intake screen. It can also mean the oil pump is worn out. You must take care not to jump to conclusions.

There are other engine conditions that can mislead you. A low or erratic vacuum reading can indicate bad valves, but if the engine has mechanical lifters, it may only mean valve clearances are out of adjustment. A leaking intake-manifold or carburetor gasket, or worn rocker bushings, rocker shafts, or adjusting screws can also cause a low or erratic vacuum reading. If you come across a problem such as this, it would be best to seek a professional opinion.

Note: Appearance items are not included in the chart since they have little to do with a car's dependability. But a thorough surface cleanup may make you feel better about your car. If your trim or bumpers are rusted or damaged, you can buy trim strips and rechromed bumpers at a reasonable price. Try cleaning paint with compound. A professional rubout with a power buffer often does wonders. In the final analysis, a paint job might be worth it if the car is in good mechanical condition.

Schedule 5. Inspect the Power System

It's quite inexpensive and a good bet to have a professional mechanic check the entire engine with an analyzer. An engine analyzer can quickly pinpoint any problems. Perform the following tests if you decide to do it yourself.

1. Check compression with a compression gauge. If it's low in one or more cylinders, the engine has either bad rings or bad valves. Squirt some oil into the bad cylinder.

    a. If the reading is higher when you recheck compression, the rings are bad.   ___good ___bad $_____

    b. If the reading is the same, the valves are bad.   ___good ___bad $_____

2. Check the oil pressure by removing the oil-pressure switch and inserting a pressure gauge. If oil pressure is not at specification, the cause may be bad rod bearings or a bad oil pump.   ___good ___bad $_____

3. Check engine vacuum with a vacuum gauge attached to the intake manifold and with the engine at operating temperature. For most engines, vacuum should be at 17 to 21 inches of mercury and hold steady. Consult the repair manual for specification for your engine.

a. If vacuum is low, the engine may have a vacuum leak or the timing may be late.

___good ___bad $_____

b. If vacuum is erratic, there may be a problem with the valve train in the camshaft, push rods, or rocker arms. Pull the engine head and check the rocker shafts, rockers, valve springs, cam lifters, and valve timing. Check the valve bores for wear at their upper ends.

___good ___bad $_____

4. Perform a power-balance test. Attach a tachometer and, with the engine at operating temperature and running at recommended idle speed, disconnect each spark plug momentarily and watch the engine rpm drop. The amount of drop should be the same for each cylinder. If not, the engine probably has an ignition, compression, or vacuum-leak problem.

___good ___bad $_____

5. Check the carburetor. If your car is more than five years old, you may need a new one.

___good ___bad $_____

6. Evaluate the results of the analyzer test and/or your tests to determine whether the engine is still good or needs to be entirely rebuilt.

___good ___bad $_____

Total $_____

How Much Will It Cost?

Go back and see if you have the skills to do any of the needed repairs. Put in parts costs for any repairs you intend to do yourself. Call a mechanic or consult *Motor Parts and Time Guide* to get estimates for all other repairs. Add up all the estimates to obtain an approximation of how much the total rebuilding project will cost you.

Unfortunately, there are no guarantees; even after rebuilding, mechanical problems can occur. But as compared to the cost of a new car or a late-model used car, rebuilding may have some advantages for you. The rebuilt car could provide you with a few more years of reasonably reliable transportation.

Index